BEYOND THE LOOM

BEYOND THE LOOM

Keys To Understanding Early Southwestern Weaving

ANN LANE HEDLUND

With an Introduction and Observations by Joe Ben Wheat

Teresa Wilkins and Diana Leonard, editors

Johnson Books: Boulder

Cover design by Molly Davis Gough
Cover photograph by Ken Abbott

Library of Congress Cataloging-in-Publication Data
Hedlund, Ann Lane, 1952–
    Beyond the loom: keys to understanding early Southwestern weaving
    / Ann Lane Hedlund: introduction and observations by Joe Ben Wheat.
       p.   cm.
    Includes bibliographical references.
    ISBN 1-55566-064-9
    1. Navajo Indians—Textile industry and fabrics. 2. Pueblo
Indians—Textile industry and fabrics. 3. Weaving—Southwest, New.
4. Navajo Indians—Textile industry and fabrics—Catalogs.
5. Pueblo Indians—Textile industry and fabrics—Catalogs.
6. Weaving—Southwest, New—Catalogs. 7. University of Colorado
(System).   Museum—Catalogs.   I. Title.
E99.N3H42   1990
746.1'4'097907478863—dc20   90-4126
                                           CIP

Printed in the United States of America by
Johnson Publishing Company
1880 South 57th Court
Boulder, Colorado 80301

Dedicated to the Weavers

of the nineteenth century
    Pueblo, Navajo, and Hispanic
    who worked from the loom
        spoke from the loom
    and left images and objects that move
        beyond the loom
and to those of the twentieth century
    who continue in the visual eloquence
    of their elders

Contents

Preface

This volume provides an introduction to the analysis, understanding and appreciation of southwestern weaving for the interested student of textiles. Three weaving cultures—the prehistoric and historic Pueblo, the Spanish Colonial, and the Navajo—left their individual and collective impact on the development of the southwestern weaving tradition that continues to the present.

Joe Ben Wheat, Curator Emeritus of the University of Colorado Museum, has developed the museum's southwestern textile collection into one of the most significant research collections in the world and, with visits to other collections, has studied more historic southwestern textiles than any other scholar.

Ann Lane Hedlund began studying the weaving and textiles of the Southwest with Joe Ben Wheat in 1973 and received her doctoral degree from the University of Colorado in 1983. Her own careful scholarship, while more often focused on modern weaving on the Navajo Reservation, reflects Joe Ben's thoughtful mentoring and teaching. As a faculty member and director of the museum studies program at Arizona State University and, fortunately for us, as a research associate at the University of Colorado Museum, Ann is influencing a new generation of students.

In the fall of 1987, Joe's infectious interest in textile research led to the formation of a museum studies seminar focused on the development of a southwestern textile exhibition that would emphasize research methodology as well as aesthetic appreciation of the textiles. The course was organized by Diana Leonard and myself. Many of the students enrolled in the seminar participated in the implementation of the exhibition and have continued in related activities such as dye analysis and collection documentation.

This volume and the exhibit entitled *Beyond the Loom: Keys to Understanding Early Southwestern Weaving*, along with a traveling exhibit component, were developed by the University of Colorado Museum. Together, they are a visual summation of the triumphs of pre-twentieth century southwestern weaving and a digest of the varied analytical techniques utilized by Wheat and his students in the study and interpretation of these textiles.

These efforts at the University of Colorado, as well as collection-based publications and catalogues on southwestern textiles by other scholars (see Further Reading at the end of this volume), reinforce the importance of museum research collections. These historically and culturally significant collections are preserved under increasingly controlled conservation conditions until new generations of scholars, asking fresh questions and using new analytical techniques, come to study them.

With the foundation established by Joe Ben Wheat and his associates, great new opportunities loom for future textile research. This volume and the exhibitions that accompany it honor Joe's scholarship and salute his friendship and inspiration to past, present, and future generations of students, colleagues, friends, and textile collectors.

Frederick W. Lange
Curator of Anthropology
University of Colorado Museum

Acknowledgments

The efforts of literally dozens of people contributed to the completion of this project. Students, collectors, textile *aficionados*, and professional colleagues have all taken an interest in the project, and the exhibition and this catalogue have benefitted from this interest.

Financial support was generously offered by the JFM Foundation, the National Endowment for the Arts, the Joe Ben Wheat Research Fund, the University of Colorado President's Fund for the Humanities, the Boulder Campus Outreach Council, and the University of Colorado Museum.

Much information in this volume was drawn from the University of Colorado Museum exhibition *Beyond the Loom: Keys to Understanding Early Southwestern Weaving*, presented to the public from 1989 to 1991 with an annual rotation of the textiles on display. The exhibit was developed by curators Joe Ben Wheat, Frederick Lange, Ann Lane Hedlund, Diana Leonard, Teresa Wilkins, and Patricia Lawrence. Initial planning of the exhibition gained considerable assistance from the students who participated in the 1987 University of Colorado Museum course, *Textile Exhibition Practicum*, supervised by Frederick Lange and Diana Leonard: Inga Calvin, Robert Carlsen, Sally Garrison, Andy Granitto, Patricia Lawrence, Jeannette Mobley, Jim Walton, Teresa Wilkins, and Lisa Yorker. The opportunity to work with the University of Colorado Museum's outstanding southwestern textile collection and to interact with Joe Ben Wheat, Ann Hedlund, and other specialists generated a wave of enthusiasm and excitement that permeated the project.

Thank you to all of the institutions and curatorial staff members who assisted Joe Ben Wheat in his extended search for documented textiles. Analyses of the dyes in many of the UCM textiles and in others studied by Wheat were conducted by Dr. David Wenger. Without Wenger's generous help, following the precedent set by Max

Saltzman, the research could not have moved forward as it did. Conservator Jeanne Brako's involvement in a conservation survey of the textile collection was a crucial element in establishing the physical requirements for each piece in the exhibit and in deciding the manner in which textiles would be mounted and displayed. The survey was made possible through a grant from the National Endowment for the Arts.

The untiring volunteer support of members of the Handweavers Guild of Boulder: Gloria Cyr, Susan Henrickson, Laurie Jennings, Anita Kindt, Elaine Smith, Chris Switzer, Maxine Wendler and Charlotte Ziebarth, with their knowledge of textile structure and skill as craftspeople, was instrumental in the preparation and stabilization of the textiles exhibited.

In addition to those persons and institutions already mentioned above, many thanks are given to the University of Colorado Museum students and volunteers whose countless hours in diverse activities led to the planning and production of both the exhibition and this catalogue. They include Ramona Avallone, Samuel Bulus, Lucile Burleson, Erin Finegan, Sally Goodman, Carol Kampert, Jeff Kopkin, Anna Marks, Jeannette Mobley, Dianne Ralston, Lisa Staten, and Kathy Williams.

Exhibition design and installation for the complex three-rotation sequence was beautifully engineered by the University of Colorado Museum exhibits department staff members David Mayo, Craig Hansen, and Andy Granitto.

Photographic skills that produced the illustrations for this volume belong to Ken Abbott of the University of Colorado Public Relations Office, and to Inga Calvin and Martin Natvig. Dorothy Goodwin provided the photograph of the Henrietta Grinnell Cole home. The illustrations were adapted from the exhibition by Craig Hansen.

A special thank you must go to the weavers of the textiles, who remain lamentably anonymous, and to the many contributors of the textiles presented in the exhibition and described here in *Selections from the UCM Collection*: William Ackard, Margery Bedinger, Lauretta Bellamy, Dr. Isabel Bittinger, Dr. Charles Bogert, Helen Borland, Fred Boschan, John Byrum, Jackson Clark, Sr., Mrs. Huber O. Croft, Charles Eagle Plume, Donnelley Erdman, Dorothy Goodwin, Mrs. Joseph P. Graves, the Graham Foundation, Mr. and Mrs. Jonathan Holstein, Mr. and Mrs. Philip Holstein, Jr., J.M. Home, Dr. John Hough, Mr. and Mrs. Erich Kohlberg, Jack and Marjorie Lambert, Carol Ann Mackay, Michael and Susan McCabe, Katherine McIntyre,

Mrs. Ellen Gary McKay, Earl H. and Lucille Morris, the Earl E. Mosley family, Robert Musser, Dorothy Odland, Pete Peterson, Mr. and Mrs. David Raffelock, Elizabeth Roberts, Hugo Rodeck, H. Medill Sarkisian, Kenneth Siebel, Edgar O. Smith, Harris A. and Lee Thompson, Eleanor Tulman-Hancock, Mr. and Mrs. Victor Walker, Joe Ben Wheat, Mark Winter, and Muriel Sibell Wolle.

Between the anonymous weaver and the known donor, there was often a trader, collector, or interested family member who saved a textile and perhaps bits of its history until it reached the museum. To all of the important links in this chain of learning, preservation, and sharing of knowledge, our greatest thanks.

Diana Leonard
Assistant Curator of Anthropology
University of Colorado Museum

Teresa Wilkins
Guest Curator
University of Colorado Museum

Boulder, Colorado
January 1990

I would like to add my own personal thanks to all of the people who collaborated on this project in its various stages; foremost, to Joe Ben Wheat who has provided inspiration, knowledge, and understanding; to Fred Lange, Diane Leonard, Teresa Wilkins, Patricia Lawrence, and other members of the *Textile Exhibition Practicum* who compiled much of the collection information included here; to David Mayo and Craig Hansen for the wonderful brainstorming sessions that helped shape and tone the entire endeavor; and to Rebecca Herr who capably guided the way to final production. I have thoroughly enjoyed working with each and every one; may every team effort have such happy results!

Ann Lane Hedlund
Department of Anthropology
Arizona State University
Tempe, Arizona

Figure 1. Patricia Lawrence, Sally Garrison, and Joe Ben Wheat examining a textile, 1987. Photo by Ken Abbott.

Introduction

During the nineteenth century, official and unofficial representatives of the formative United States moved ever westward across North America in pursuit of "Manifest Destiny." As they moved they came into greater and greater contact with many Indian tribes of the West. Frequently, they vied for commercial exploitation and settlement with some of the European nations. In the Southwest, for instance, they encountered the already established American colonies of Spain. In the 1820s the U.S. opened up a trade route to Santa Fe, known as the Santa Fe Trail. By 1846, this trade, which had begun as a trickle, had burgeoned into a major enterprise. The Mexican War, fought at least in part to preserve this trade, resulted in the United States taking over nearly all of the southwestern corner of North America. With the territory came the Spanish colonists, the several Pueblo Indian nations, and the Apaches, Navajos, and other Native Americans who lived along the western and southern rivers.

The new Americans—merchants, military, and settlers—found that many of the peoples of the Southwest were makers of desirable goods, such as pottery, metals, and textiles. The Pueblo peoples, who had been weavers for some two thousand years, were no longer making large quantities of woven articles for sale to the Spanish as they had for many centuries before, but the descendants of the Spanish settlers along the Rio Grande were major suppliers of cloth and blankets of several kinds to California and northern Mexico, to some of the Plains Indians, several of the Apache tribes, the Utes, the Navajos, and to the newly arrived Americans. By this time, the Navajo, who had learned to weave from the Pueblos sometime in the 1600s, had become dominant figures in southwestern weaving. If the Navajo woven products did not match the Spanish fabrics in quantity, they clearly made up for it in terms of quality. When common Spanish blankets sold for two dollars and the finest Hispanic copies of Saltillo and Navajo sarapes sold for twenty, the fine Navajo sarapes brought fifty to a hundred dollars.

Many of these blankets of the mid-nineteenth century found their way into the hands of the Americans of New Mexico and Arizona, but many more were sent East by early merchants and settlers as curios for their families and friends. Military personnel had blankets woven for their superiors or collected for museums of the day. Other government people, such as the explorers and surveyors, collected blankets. Through the years most of these pieces lost their provenience as families died out or lost their connections with the West, but a surprising number of them maintained the slender threads that tied them to their original time and place. It is these fabrics which form the major anchors in our studies today.

If most of the earlier blankets came into collections inadvertently, during the latter part of the nineteenth century deliberate collecting became the fashion. An "Indian Room" or "Indian Corner" became an institution in the Victorian household. Collecting became a passion with many wealthy men, and it is from these collectors that major increments in present-day public textile collections have derived. For the most part, these accumulations have gone to major museums in the eastern and midwestern United States, but some went West or stayed in the Southwest.

Meanwhile, other agencies were also involved in the study of "Vanishing Americans" and in collecting the articles of material culture which are the basis of most research today. Even major art museums collected American Indian art until about 1910 when it lost its status as art and returned to the status of curio. Nevertheless, institutions with interest in anthropology as such (the great natural history museums, for example) continued to amass quantities of materials against the day when they would no longer be made, and individuals working in the West continued to bring or send home articles to remember their stay.

The opening of the railroads brought travelers. To cater to their interests, curio shops sprang up over the Southwest. Fred Harvey, concessionaire to the Santa Fe Railroad, became a dominant force in buying and selling Native American and Spanish arts, especially textiles, which had become diversified for other uses around the house. The rug industry that developed around the turn of the century now was the main thrust of the weavers, and pillow tops, chair throws, and runners proliferated. Only the saddle blanket continued to be woven for its direct use by the Navajo.

Early writers on southwestern weaving, such as U.S. Hollister (*The Navajo and his Blanket*), G.W. James (*Indian Blankets and their Makers*), and Charles Amsden (*Navajo Weaving; its Technic and its History*), relied heavily on traders' tales and, sometimes, on their own imagination or opinion to tell their stories. Nevertheless, Amsden and his contemporary, H.P. Mera, did begin to analyze southwestern weaving and to distinguish its salient visual and technical characteristics.

Public exhibitions of Native American art began to appear with increasing frequency after the 1930s. Many of the exhibitions were focused primarily on the aesthetics of the earlier blankets and of contemporary rugs. Theme exhibits developed in which textiles of one group, such as Spanish Colonial or the Hopi Pueblos, were featured. It is in this context that this catalogue and the 1989-1991 exhibit at the University of Colorado Museum takes place. The theme is the how and why of southwestern weaving, and the historic framework that binds the several traditions together. The story is about the interplay of the various weaving groups, the growth of design styles, the use of exotic as well as indigenous materials, and how these have, through time, created a magnificent heritage of southwestern weaving among the Pueblo, Spanish, and Navajo.

Joe Ben Wheat
Curator Emeritus
University of Colorado Museum

Beyond The Loom

 Once the weaver's task is complete and the finished product is taken from the loom—what happens to it? Beyond the loom, fabrics become many things: garments, bedding, floor coverings, trade items, and curios. Often such handwoven textiles end up in museum collections to be preserved, displayed, and studied.

Many Southwestern blankets in museum collections are approaching or exceed one hundred years in age. Some were made just yesterday. Each may provide reference materials for us to learn about the people who made and originally used them, and about the times in which they were made.

Whether intended or not, textiles become emblems of the people who made and used them. Clues about society and history are encoded in the fibers, yarns, dyes, and weave structures of each blanket or rug and revealed through research. The structure of the textile may suggest when, where, and how it was made; worn spots, frayed edges, or alterations may provide insights into how it was used. As objects of careful study, textiles can represent interesting people, places, and times.

Dr. Joe Ben Wheat is considered a pioneer in the study of nineteenth century textiles from the American Southwest. Through his research, he has developed significant new insights into the weaving traditions. In particular, his research has revealed the importance of cross-cultural relationships among Pueblo, Navajo, and Hispanic weavers and the products of their looms.

The main essay in this book shows some ways in which southwestern blankets have moved beyond the loom and are studied. It details the dynamic work of Dr. Wheat and emphasizes the importance of research on museum collections. The comparative chart that follows the essay outlines some of the salient traits for southwestern textile study and indicates how they may be used to distinguish the cultural origins of different fabrics. The specific descriptions and Dr. Wheat's commentary that accompany the selected listing of southwestern textiles from the University of Colorado Museum collection further develop the idea that careful observations, scientific testing, and historical documentation combine to increase our understanding of individual fabrics as well as textile history. A glossary is provided for reference, and a list of suggestions for further reading is included for those who want more detailed historical information. Since an adequate description of the historical development of textile production in the Southwest is beyond the scope of this book, the reader may want to refer especially to the writings of scholars Joe Ben Wheat and Kate Peck Kent. Through the assemblage of information presented here, we hope that readers learn how information about southwestern weaving is acquired and interpreted, adding new perspectives to the understanding of the Pueblo, Navajo, and Spanish Colonial textile traditions.

Keys to Understanding:
Joe Ben Wheat's
Southwestern Textile Survey

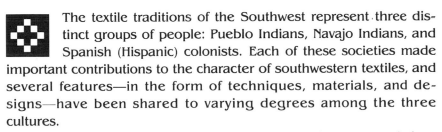 The textile traditions of the Southwest represent three distinct groups of people: Pueblo Indians, Navajo Indians, and Spanish (Hispanic) colonists. Each of these societies made important contributions to the character of southwestern textiles, and several features—in the form of techniques, materials, and designs—have been shared to varying degrees among the three cultures.

The research of Joe Ben Wheat has revealed important relationships between Pueblo, Navajo, and Spanish Colonial weavers and the products of their looms, especially in the nineteenth century. In 1972, he embarked on a study to analyze and photograph as many fully documented textiles in public collections across the nation as possible, and to compare their physical traits with historic written records. The main objective was to establish a key for their identification. The key would represent a basic scheme to (a) distinguish among the three textile traditions and (b) provide relative dates for previously undated textiles.

With a systematic approach that reflects his background in archaeology, Wheat developed a timeline for textiles woven in the Southwest based upon materials, techniques, design styles, and historical correlations. Many earlier assumptions regarding native weaving were challenged. Today, a much clearer picture of the evolution of southwestern textile production can be drawn because of Wheat's pioneering work. Curators, collectors, and other researchers now have a standard set of tools with which to identify Native American and Hispanic fabrics. This essay describes the approach that Wheat used in order to establish a scheme for identifying and dating textiles.

JOE BEN WHEAT

The training and experience that Joe Ben Wheat received as an archaeologist working with prehistoric cultures of the Southwest served him well in pursuing a research project focusing on more recent historic and ethnographic materials. He studied under Alfred L. Kroeber and Robert Lowie, and earned a B.A. in anthropology at the University of California, Berkeley, in 1937. He did graduate work under Emil Haury and Edward H. Spicer at the University of Arizona, and received an M.A. (1949) and Ph.D. (1953). Among other things, both universities emphasized the skills and tools required to make systematic analyses of artifacts. Wheat's major archaeological research, such as his projects at the prehistoric Jurgens, Olsen-Chubbuck, and Yellow Jacket sites, repeatedly points out the relevance of artifact studies in archaeology and, more generally, in anthropology.

Wheat arrived at the University of Colorado Museum (UCM) in 1953 as Curator of Anthropology, and retired as Curator Emeritus in 1986. In the intervening years he built up the ethnographic holdings from less than one hundred specimens to a collection of over 15,000 pieces with worldwide coverage. The UCM archaeological collections, established largely by Earl Morris in the early part of this century, have also grown considerably under Wheat's direction. In the process of expanding the UCM anthropology collections, Wheat discovered just how little was actually understood about southwestern textiles. He proceeded to acquire as many specimens with known histories as possible through solicitation of donations and by select purchases. By the 1980s the textiles at UCM numbered close to five hundred, and today they represent an extremely significant assemblage for study, making this one of the top ten collections of such material. Wheat, however, had already recognized a decade earlier that no one institution could possibly hold the entire key to understanding the development of the southwestern textile traditions. A broader data base drawn from the collections at many institutions was needed.

THE RESEARCH PROJECT

Wheat designed the textile survey in response to the need for a greater understanding of the nature of southwestern weaving and a better chronological framework. His original research goals were to determine whether textiles of the Southwest contain particular physical characteristics that lend themselves to identifying cultural and temporal origins and, if so, to establish which of those characteristics were associated with what cultures and time periods. In order to construct this key for identification, Wheat's objectives became the study of as many well-documented textiles as possible, and the subsequent comparison of their recorded features with ethnohistoric materials.

A first-hand examination of literally thousands of textiles became possible through a sabbatical year survey of selected museum collections in 1972. Utilizing the Museum Directory of the American Association of Museums, Wheat contacted all institutions that listed southwestern weaving among their holdings. More than forty museums answered his request for further information. A ten-month itinerary, covering the U.S., Canada, England, and Sweden, was established on the basis of this preliminary survey.

From September 1972 to June 1973, Wheat visited approximately fifty museums and a few private collections, viewed over 3500 textiles from the native Southwest, and closely analyzed and photographed about 2000 of those fabrics. Pieces selected for close examination were chosen because they were accompanied by documentary evidence of their cultural origins or subsequent ownership. Over the next decade, data from this early work were extended through the analysis of other textiles and through further archival work. In the early 1980s, the identification of a series of significant dyes was accomplished with the aid of Dr. David Wenger, then associated with the Univerity of Colorado Medical School in Denver.

The following four sections detail the major thrusts of Wheat's data-gathering process: the review of collection records, the description of the textiles, ethnohistorical research, and the identification of dyes.

Collection Histories

Basic records for the collections that Wheat surveyed were found in museum files: accession ledgers, catalogue cards, donor and registration files, and various other forms of documentation maintained routinely by museums. Accompanying information included notes about original manufacture, initial acquisition by a collector, and other associations with people, places, events, or dates. Correspondence by early collectors was sometimes helpful in reconstructing the latest possible date for manufacture and special circumstances sur-

Figure 2. Henrietta Grinnell Cole house. Collection of Dorothy Goodwin.

rounding acquisition. Annotations on museum catalogue records by earlier scholars—Charles Amsden and H.P. Mera, for instance—were occasionally revealing. Sometimes a number or code written on a textile indicated a previous owner and yielded important associations, such as those textiles collected and numbered by George Heye at the turn of the century but found in museums other than his own Museum of the American Indian (Heye Foundation).

Documentation generally refers to written information, although some scholars, especially those working in museums, use the term to cover any type of recorded evidence. Photographs, occasionally from the original collector, were another documentary medium that provided additional context and corroboration for written information. The photographs of Henrietta Grinnell Cole's home, decorated with her collection at the turn of the century, provide visual clues to the earlier history of her textiles, now in the University of Colorado

Museum (Figure 2). In another example, a photograph in the collections of the National Gallery of Art shows George Catlin, the well-known painter of the West, with one Navajo and two Rio Grande Spanish sarapes collected by him on a 1854 trip through Arizona and New Mexico. Connecting such photographs with actual museum specimens can be a thrilling challenge.

According to Wheat's survey, the textile with the earliest known date is a blanket collected near Veracruz, Mexico, in 1847 by a Colonel Burton Randall when he served in the Mexican War (see Plate 1). Other complete blankets have been documented to subsequent decades, but only archaeological fragments and a very few whole textiles remain to represent earlier years. This knowledge is the result of careful sleuth work on Wheat's part. When he first encountered the blanket in a private collection, its history consisted of a tale that it had been acquired when Randall was in Mexico during the 1840s (see Figure 3). Through a gratifying search of the military records in the National Archives in Washington, Wheat confirmed that Randall was indeed stationed in Mexico during 1847. Now in the collection of the University of Colorado Museum, the blanket is notable not because it is the oldest in absolute terms (there are undoubtedly older specimens, but without documentation) nor the most visually striking, but because of the historical confirmation of its age.

Well-known names in the exploration of the West and in early contacts with American Indians have surfaced in the search for documented textiles: John Wesley Powell, the famous explorer of the Grand Canyon and first director of the Smithsonian's Bureau of American Ethnology, collected Navajo blankets and mantas in the mid-1870s. Two women's shawls collected by Powell are included in the UCM collections. Although some of these are in poor physical condition, they are nevertheless extremely important because of their illustrious collector and the documented collection dates. Noted writer and collector Charles F. Lummis acquired a variety of blankets in the 1880s. These, along with similar examples from a number of other collections, provide a baseline for understanding weaving of this decade.

Several textiles included in the study were associated with important historical events. For instance, a Navajo sarape, known as the Chief White Antelope blanket (named after its original Arapahoe owner), was acquired by an Army officer at the 1864 Sand Creek Massacre in Colorado. Now in the collections of the School of American Research in Santa Fe, this blanket, along with others in Wheat's sur-

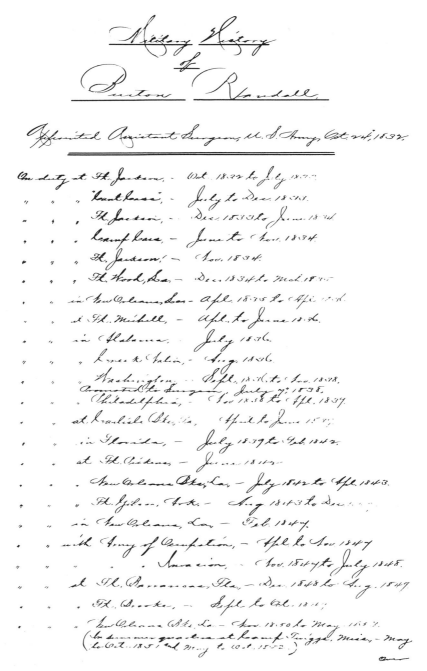

Figure 3. Documentation for collector of the "Randall sarape."

On duty at Ft. Gibson, Ark, – June 1853 to July 1854
"   "   " Carlisle Bks., Pa. – Sept. 1857 to Oct. 1861.
"   "   " Gul. Hospl. Annapolis, Md. – Oct. 1861 – July 1862.
"   "   " Ft. Hamilton, N.Y.H. – July 1862 to Mch. 1866.
"   "   " Ft. Trumbull, Conn. – Apl. 1866 to Sept. 1867.
On sick leave of absence from Sept. 1867 to
Sept. 1869.   Retired from active service Oct. 19th, 1869.

———————

Brevetted, Lieut. Colonel, Mch. 13th, 1865, for
faithful and meritorious service during the
war.

———————

Died February 5th, 1886.

Official,

D. L. Huntington
Surgeon, U. S. Army.

S. G. O.
May 24th, 1886.

vey, has provided the material and stylistic basis upon which several other visually similar textiles have been identified and dated.[*]

The reliability and accuracy of collection histories must be considered seriously, and Wheat's study provides numerous examples of the need to cross-check collectors' stories against independent sources of information. The vagaries of memory, problems in consistent recordkeeping, family rivalries, and other potentially biasing phenomena can hinder the accuracy of collection-related stories. Wheat sought to identify and, when possible, to reconcile any contradictions between collection histories and the physical evidence. For example, it was originally supposed that William Nicholson Grier collected a series of blankets between 1846 and 1861 before he left his post in New Mexico (Wheat 1977:431). However, certain materials and designs in these blankets did not appear in other documented textiles until about ten years later. Wheat's subsequent search of the U.S. military archives showed that Grier returned to the Southwest as commanding officer of Fort Union during 1869-70, thus documenting the collection more accurately to the late 1860s and correcting previous information.

Describing the Textiles

The central objective of Wheat's extensive textile survey was to provide systematic and reliable descriptions of the textiles with verifiable documentation so that their physical features could be compared to each other and against the historic record. Ultimately, the goal was to be able to compare these known textiles with others lacking documentation. The process of assigning a culture and time period to unknown materials began, therefore, with an accurate physical description. For descriptions of the technical terms that are incorporated into the following discussion, please refer to the Glossary.

Physical examination. Descriptions for each textile were recorded on a standardized form in order to ensure similar kinds of information from different textiles and different institutions (Figure 4). Features include the overall size of the fabric, structure of the weave, side and end selvage finishes, corner details, presence and frequency

---

[*] See Kent (1985:36-37) for a discussion of this blanket and a related piece also in the School of American Research collections.

University of Colorado Museum   *Textiles*

Type: Sarape, small - medium poncho   Catalogue No. —
Culture: Navajo   Owner: Fred Barclan
Weave: Plain tapestry
Selvage: warp : 2 3-ply
        weft : 2 3-ply - joined at ¼ but both ends are 5 wound/ corners missing

Dimensions: Thread Count:
  Length: 47⅝ inches; 121 cm.   Warp: 11 per inch (2.5 cm)
  Width: 30½ inches; 77.5 cm.   Weft: 44 per inch (2.5 cm) handspun
        29¼ .. 74.5 unr   68 x 24 " " raveled

Lazy lines: a few - tight + short
Materials: handspun + raveled

Fiber	Type of Yarn	Spin	Twist	Ply	Color	Dye
warp -wool	handspun, fine	2	.	(	white	none
weft ① wool	handspun . med	2	-	(	white	none
② "	" "	2	-	1	dk red blue	Indigo
③ "	" "	2	-	1	dk gold	Vegetal
④ "	" "	2	-	(	med "	"
⑤ "	" "	2	-	1	blue green	" + Indigo
⑥ "	" "	2	-	(	yellow green	" "
⑦ "	raveled fine .35	3	II	2	crimson	cochineal
⑧ "	" med .5	2	"	2	chocolate brown faded to dk tan	vegetal ?
Selvage warp wool	handspun	2	S	3	dk med blue	Indigo
weft "	"	2	S	3	" " "	"

Description: Small childs blanket, white ground with center and end decorative panels - White woven by compound stripe cluster in red and brown - Five poncho-like stripe flank center and end panel

Center slit cut with wefts and across warps had silk tape binding to convert blanket into poncho

Date of Manufacture: Date of Collection: c 18 47
History/Remarks

Photo: Color   Analysis by: JBW   Date: 5/16/78

Figure 4. Dr. Joe Ben Wheat's textile analysis form for the "Randall sarape."

of lazy lines, yarn construction (type of fibers, commercial vs. hand-production, texture, color, spin/ply configuration and count), and any other structural aspects that were noted during examination.

Because it was not apparent at the outset which traits might emerge as important diagnostics, the physical aspects of each textile were analyzed as thoroughly as possible. Through time, it became clear that certain features were extremely important in identifying textiles, while others appeared less useful. As the study progressed, corner finishes, for example, were recognized as important indicators of Pueblo, Navajo, or Hispanic origins. Consequently more space on the analysis sheet was allotted to their description during the course of the study.

Museum records could not always be relied upon and first-hand inspection became extremely important to making accurate descriptions. For instance, many weft counts (threads per inch) recorded in museum files and in publications proved to be wrong because earlier investigators had failed to count the weft threads on both faces of the fabric. Descriptions of colors (the varied shades of red, for example) differed from one catalogue entry to another. Even the identification of wool versus cotton was often unreliable and so had to be ascertained for each piece directly.

Style categories. Notes were made regarding the overall layout of the design; the numbers, scale, and types of motifs; the color scheme; and any other particulars that would allow Wheat to distinguish one blanket from another. From these reference points, groups with similar styles were discerned. Many styles had previously been described, such as three main phases of chief blankets, and others such as Moqui stripes and Vallero star patterns, but systematic note-taking allowed for finer distinctions in many previously unstudied styles—for instance, the different rhythms in Pueblo, Navajo, and Spanish striped blankets and variations in Navajo women's banded blankets.

Photography. Approximately three thousand color slides of the analyzed textiles were made. Photographs were taken in many different settings and under widely divergent conditions. Yet, because of a special portable hanging system developed by Wheat, results were relatively uniform and provided a good way of comparing textiles in widely separated collections. These slides were later used for triggering the memory when reviewing analysis forms, for sorting when making stylistic comparisons and, ultimately, for selecting prospective illustrations for publication.

Ethnohistorical Research

Ethnohistory is generally considered to be the study of ethnic people through the use of written, i.e. historic, records (in contrast, for example, to ethnology—the study of ethnic people through anthropological observation, interviews and other methods involving fieldwork). In addition to the collection records accompanying individual textiles that were discussed above, many other historical sources are available for the study of early weaving. Ethnohistoric evidence, that is, the written record, has sometimes confirmed the physical evidence, sometimes contradicted anecdotal information or erroneous "documentation," and generally has provided a new dimension to the understanding of the textile traditions of the Southwest.

A number of writers provide us with firsthand descriptions of the early Southwest and its inhabitants. Foremost are several Spanish chroniclers of the eighteenth century (see, for instance, Bailey and Haggard 1942; Troncoso 1788; Hackett 1937; Hill 1940). Anglo observers recorded the southwestern scene of the mid-nineteenth century, including commentary on textile production and use (Bartlett 1965; Gregg 1844). Later in the century, Matilda Coxe Stevenson and Frank Cushing, ethnologists for the Bureau of American Ethnology, documented textile production at Zuni Pueblo (Stevenson 1904, 1987). Washington Matthews, a major in the U.S. Army Medical Corps and an amateur ethnologist, made a description of the tools and handwoven fabrics of the Navajo (1884) and reported on native dyes and design styles (1893, 1900, 1904).

Unpublished federal, state, and private archives were also used in Wheat's search for relevant information. In 1975 Wheat worked in the U.S. National Archives in Washington, making notes from those documents not available on microfilm, and selecting fifty reels of microfilmed documents that would later be transcribed and further studied. Particularly interesting were materials from the U.S. Indian Service (now known as the Bureau of Indian Affairs), including correspondence received from the Indian agents in the field and files on Indian issues in New Mexico. The New Mexico State Records Center and Archives, which contains the Spanish, Mexican, and Territorial Archives of New Mexico, as well as U.S. census reports and the

Archives of the Archdiocese of Santa Fe, were also fruitful sources of information.

Wheat studied ledgers and trade invoices of Spanish and Mexican traders dating from the seventeenth century through the 1860s, and the ledgers, invoices, letters, annuity records, and other documents pertaining to the Indian traders of the last half of the nineteenth century. The documents of private trading concerns such as Hubbell Trading Post (in the University of Arizona Special Collections) and the American Fur Company proved to be rich resources, as did the Business Archives at the University of Texas at Austin.

These ethnohistoric records yielded information concerning the quantities and types of tools and raw materials provided to the Navajo through barter and purchase with Mexican, Hispanic, and Anglo traders and through their annuity provisions from the U.S. government. For instance, the purchases made by the Navajo Agent for the Navajo Indians are recorded in the U.S. National Archives, providing a fascinating annual accounting of dyes, yarns, and fabrics that were available in the 1860s, 1870s and 1880s. Breed names and numbers of sheep sent to the Southwest were documented. Some of the sources, types, and amounts of bayeta fabrics are indicated. The amounts, types and colors of commercial yarns supplied to the Navajo are recorded as well.

Another productive avenue was to seek records of certain government employees who collected early textiles that have since found their way into museum collections. Frank Hamilton Cushing, Washington Matthews, James and Matilda Coxe Stevenson, John Russell Bartlett, Samuel Woodhouse—all were connected to the government in some way, and all collected southwestern materials with associated documentation. Many of their records, including lists of objects that were collected, are housed in the National Anthropological Archives and registration records of the Smithsonian Institution. Certain collectors such as John Wesley Powell were well-known figures in the American West, others like Thomas Ewing, a government contractor who lived in Tucson in the 1870s, required some detective work to identify more fully. A large sarape in the University of Colorado Museum collections has the initials "TE" woven prominently into its center and may have been woven for Thomas Ewing (Plate 3). Its materials and style attest to a date in the early 1870s. In fact, Wheat has shown that this blanket contains every color and type of commercial yarn known to have been distributed to the Navajo on December 25, 1870, according to the annuity records studied by

Wheat. This particular combination of yarns was not previously nor subsequently issued to the Navajo for their weaving.

There are serious problems with relying too heavily on documentary sources without some cross-checking. Fully aware of this, Wheat has tried to qualify ambiguous information and to reconcile potential discrepancies in the records. Traders in the Mexican territory, for instance, were required to pay duty on imported goods, thus their recordkeeping was not always reliable: ". . . there was, apparently, considerable falsification of these documents, with joint connivance of trader and customs inspector, especially in the early years of the trade (Wheat n.d.:121-122). While hundreds of pounds of cotton, silk, and wool yarns appear as standard items in these invoices, the figures represent minimum amounts only.

Dye Identification

Materials scientists and other specialists can play an important role in identifying dyes used in textiles. While the physical examination of documented textiles and the archival search for corroborating information could be accomplished without outside help, certain aspects of the survey such as dye testing required collaboration with specialists. Their help proved to be a valuable key to identifying textiles of certain time periods.

Following Wheat's museum survey and early analyses, it became apparent that absolute identification of certain dyed yarns, especially the reds, might be useful. Wheat explored various methods to test dyes, but had little success until Max Saltzman, Research Specialist at the Institute of Geophysics and Planetary Physics, University of California at Los Angeles, became involved. In the mid-1970s Saltzman determined the colorants in fifty-five historic Hispanic blankets for the Museum of International Folk Art (Saltzman and Fisher 1979). As a consequence, standard spectrophotometric curves in the ultraviolet and visible light range were established for a number of southwestern dyestuffs. These could be used to compare against curves from unknown colorants.

In 1978, Saltzman conducted a pilot study for Wheat, in which ten samples from the University of Colorado Museum collection were tested using a technique called solution spectrophotometry. In addition to the expected presence of cochineal and/or aniline dyes in most late nineteenth century fabrics, the red insect dye, lac, was discovered in the trade cloth of a Navajo war shirt and in the raveled yarns of a classic blanket, both from the early nineteenth century (Plate 4). While cochineal and lac are both derived from insects, cochineal (*Dactylopius coccus,* formerly known as *Coccus cacti*) comes from the New World and lac (*Laccifer lacca,* formerly known as *Coccus lacca*) comes from India. A third insect dye, kermes (*Kermes* sp.) from Asia, has not been found in southwestern fabrics to date.

Once the usefulness of such dye testing was confirmed, samples from a carefully selected series of documented textiles were requested from a number of museums. Although all museums ultimately complied with the request, because the sampling required the removal of a minute quantity of colored fiber from each textile, it was necessary in certain cases to receive full board approval before samples were taken. Spectrophotometric analysis was conducted by Dr. David Wenger. From 1981 through 1983, tests were performed on nearly five hundred samples.

IDENTIFYING CULTURES AND DATES

Wheat's methods for identifying and dating southwestern weaving were established by comparing information, as described above, from historical records and the objects themselves. The detailed compilation of individual textile histories, design styles, materials, and dyes for known textiles was followed by the comparison of these features between different cultures and through different time periods.

Known dates for specific textiles were tabulated and cross-referenced with the occurrences of various physical features: weave structures, selvage techniques, corner finishes, lazy lines, fibers, colors, dyes, yarns, twists and plies, and so forth. Data on aspects of design—motifs, layout, and color schemes—as well as technical traits were graphed. Individual as well as group tables were made for the various functional and stylistic types such as ponchos, sarapes, chief blankets, wedge weaves, two-piece dresses, and saddle blankets. Documented pieces were highlighted throughout the tables as a way of creating a timeline for the noted physical characteristics.

Identifying a textile from its materials, weave, or design alone would be difficult and likely inaccurate; it is the series of related diagnostic features that is significant. Although Wheat's entire identification scheme cannot be presented here, a brief description of some of the results will suggest the nature and usefulness of his findings. A comparison chart of southwestern textile traits briefly summarizes this information (see pp. 35–36).

Styles. Differences in design and style have long been noted as important factors in identifying southwestern textiles. Due to the large sample size of visual images compiled by Wheat, finer distinctions in the treatment of woven patterns by Pueblo, Navajo, and Hispanic weavers were recognized. Specific motifs, such as crosses, terraced diamonds, or eight-pointed stars, often are linked with certain regions and time periods. For example, Saltillo-influenced serrate designs generally are not found in Navajo weaving prior to the Bosque Redondo internment in 1863. The rhythm of certain striped or banded patterns, the layout of bordered designs, and a variety of other aesthetic cues may contribute to the identification or dating of a textile.

At the same time, the fickle nature of design must be acknowledged. More than materials or techniques, graphic designs can be shared between different peoples and can appear in different time periods. Thus designs should often be regarded as reinforcing rather than decisive features. It is important to consider all aspects in an integrated manner instead of relying upon design as a single identifying criterion.

Construction. Important distinctions between Pueblo, Navajo, and Hispanic selvage systems were suspected in the early stages of the research, but the real value of such study was demonstrated when information was charted out and correlated with the documentary evidence. The nature of the corner finishes, the presence or absence of lazy lines, the proportion of warp to weft counts (i.e., the spacing of the yarns and consequent density of the fabric), and many other construction features also had to be put into perspective against historic information and other evidence before being used to identify unknown textiles.

> . . . research has shown that there were fairly consistent differences in various technical features which usually enable the student to distinguish between textiles woven by Navajo, Pueblo, and Spanish weavers. Spanish blankets were usually woven in two pieces which were then sewn together, or which had doubled warps at the center, while Pueblo and Navajo textiles were always of one piece. Indian weavers used single-

ply warps, while the Spanish used two-ply warps. The ends of Spanish blankets had warps which extended beyond the web and which were tied into fringes or tied off with various kinds of knots, while Indian blankets had selvage cords along both ends and sides. Among the Pueblo weavers these generally consisted of three cords of two plies each, only loosely joined at the corners, while the Navajo usually used two cords of three plies each to form the selvages and joined them tightly at the corners. Sometimes Spanish blankets have pseudo-selvage cords added by repairers, but they are not original. Navajo blankets were frequently woven a small area at a time, leaving diagonal "lazy lines" in the web, while such lines are rarely found in Pueblo weaving.

Spanish and Navajo blankets of all kinds are usually woven in tapestry weave, including the tapestry twills of the Navajo, while the Pueblos preferred plain weave or plain twills both diagonal and diamond (Wheat, in Mera and Wheat 1978:6).

Materials. Raw materials and types of yarn proved to be important diagnostics. Physical changes such as the differing textures, contrasting diameters, and varied grease contents of handspun wools were correlated with archival information about the introduction of different sheep breeds into the Southwest, ranging from the Andalusian churro to the Spanish merino, French rambouillet, and others.

As the wool changed over the years, the character of the yarns spun from them changed also, from the naturally worsted yarns of churro wool to the coarse, greasy woolen yarns from the mixed breeds. It is usually possible to determine, by an examination of the native spun yarns in a blanket, its approximate place in time, an approximation that may be refined by observing other features such as the associated raveled or commercial yarns, the dyes, and the designs (Wheat n.d.:43).

The analysis of raveled yarns has resulted in particularly important information for dating textiles. Once thought to be a relatively simple handful of yarns from imported cloths, the varied nature of raveled materials was revealed by Wheat both through technical analysis and through archival research. Raveled yarns may be either s-spun or z-spun, smooth or fuzzy in texture, straight or spiralled in structure, colored with natural (plant or animal) or synthetic (aniline) dyes. They were used singly and in groups, and also in cut strips. Further differences were discovered when the red dyes used on many raveled yarns were tested and proved to be lac, cochineal, or anilines. Trade records attest to many foreign sources and many types of fabric that were involved in the Southwest market.

The analysis of commercial yarns that were not raveled helped establish time sequences, again, especially when used along with archival data. Texture differences between the early Zephyr, rare Saxony, and more common Germantown yarns occurred at specific times. Even more obvious, a change from 3-ply to 4-ply Germantown yarns was noted in textiles of the 1860s and 1870s.

> Throughout the Spanish period, commercial yarns were standard items of commerce in New Mexico. Wool and silk yarns from Europe and China, and from Mexico itself reached New Mexico through the annual supply trains and the trade fairs. After 1821, the supply of yarns increasingly came across the Santa Fe Trail. Saxony yarns, a fine 3-ply spun from Saxony Merino sheep, dyed with indigo, cochineal, madder, and other commercial dyes of the day, was one of the main yarns imported, and while it was commonly used in Spanish-American weaving for decorative detail, it does not seem to have been much used by the Navajo until late Classic times, that is, from about 1845 to 1865. During the period, it was employed fairly often, and a number of blankets were made entirely from Saxony. After the commercialization of aniline dyes in 1856, another commercial yarn made its appearance among the Navajo. This was "Early Germantown" yarn, like Saxony, of three plies, but dyed with aniline dyes in a wide variety of colors. Most of these yarns are either very dull yellows, greens, browns, and lavenders, or highly saturated orange-reds, blues, and yellows, but of little luster. They were in use by 1864 and continued in use until about 1875, when they were increasingly displaced by 4-ply "Germantown" yarns of the same character (Wheat 1977:422-423).

Dyes. The results of the dye tests, even though restricted primarily to the red portion of the spectrum, were extremely gratifying. Not only were unexpected dyes such as lac revealed, but previously unidentified combinations of dyes (notably, cochineal and lac used together in varying proportions) were discovered. Most importantly, certain dyes correlated quite well with specific time periods and with yarn types and design styles:

> . . . lac was the most common red dye from the late 1700s to the early 1860s when lac was almost completely replaced by cochineal. Lac has an overwhelming association with fine-threaded, S-spun yarns raveled from worsted cloths, more than 95 percent of all early raveled yarn falling in this category. The shift from worsted yarns to woolen yarns beginning about 1860 corresponds to the shift from lac to cochineal dye. Except for small amounts of locally woven bayeta, and perhaps some from Mexico or Spain, all early bayeta was a worsted cloth dyed with lac. (Wheat n.d.:72)

THE FUTURE

Through Wheat's methodical research, the basic tools for understanding early southwestern textiles now exist for future application. Wheat and other scholars will continue to refine and extend the identification process according to new data recovered from museum collections and from archives. With established ways to determine the origins of a textile, curators and collectors may now correct their records, update identifications, and critically review collection histories. This paves the way for future research that is more accurate and creates important keys that open the gates to better understanding.

REFERENCES CITED

Bailey, Carroll H., and J.V. Haggard
  1942   *Three New Mexico Chronicles*. Albuquerque, NM: The Quivira Society.

Bartlett, John Russell
  1965   *Personal Narrative of Explorations and Incidents of Texas, New Mexico, California, Sonora and Chihuahua, 1850-1853*. Reprint of the 1854 manuscript. Chicago: Rio Grande Press.

Fisher, Nora, and Joe Ben Wheat
  1979   The Materials of Southwestern Weaving. In *Spanish Textile Tradition of New Mexico and Colorado*. Nora Fisher, ed. Pp. 196-200. Santa Fe, NM: Museum of International Folk Art and Museum of New Mexico Press.

Gregg, Josiah
  1844   *Commerce on the Prairies*. New York.

Hackett, Charles W
  1937   *Historical Documents Relating to New Mexico, Nueva Vizcaya, and Approaches Thereto, to 1773*. 3 vols. Washington, DC: Carnegie Institution.

Hedlund, Ann Lane
  1989   The Study of Nineteenth Century Southwestern Textiles. In *Perspectives on Anthropological Collections from the American Southwest*. A.L. Hedlund, ed. Anthropological Research Papers 40. Pp. 121-138. Tempe: Arizona State University.

Hill, W.W.
  1940   Some Navaho Culture Changes during Two Centuries (With a translation of the early eighteenth century Rabal manuscript). In *Essays in Historical Anthropology of North America*, Smithsonian Miscellaneous Collections 100. Pp. 395-415. Washington, D.C.

Matthews, Washington
  1893   Navajo Dye Stuffs. *Smithsonian Institution Annual Report for 1891*. Pp. 613-615. Washington, D.C.: U.S. Government Printing Office.

  1884   Navajo Weavers. *Third Annual Report of the Bureau of American Ethnology, 1880-1882*. Pp. 375-391. Washington, DC: U.S. Government Printing Office.

  1900   A Two-Faced Navaho Blanket. *American Anthropologist* n.s. 2:638-642.

  1904   The Navaho Yellow Dye. *American Anthropologist* n.s. 6:194.

Mera, H.P., and Joe Ben Wheat
  1978   *The Alfred I. Barton Collection of Southwestern Textiles*, revised edition. Coral Gables, FL: The Lowe Art Museum, University of Miami.

Saltzman, Max, and Nora Fisher
   1979   The Dye Analysis; Introductory Remarks. In *Spanish Textile Tradition of New Mexico and Colorado*. Nora Fisher, ed. Pp. 212-216. Santa Fe, NM: Museum of International Folk Art and Museum of New Mexico Press.

Stevenson, Matilda Coxe
   1904   The Zuni Indians: Their Mythology, Esoteric Fraternities, and Ceremonies. *23rd Annual Report of the Bureau of American Ethnology, 1901-1902*. pp. 1-634. Washington, D.C.: U.S. Government Printing Office.

Stevenson, Matilda Coxe (Richard V.N. Ahlstrom and Nancy J. Parezo, eds.)
   1987   Dress and Adornment of the Pueblo Indians. *The Kiva* 52(4):275-312.

Troncoso, Vicente
   1788   Report to Don Fernando de la Concha, Santa Fe, April 12, (Manuscript, copy in file of the Navajo Tribal Research Library, Window Rock, AZ).

Wheat, Joe Ben
   1976a   Navajo Textiles. In *Fred Harvey Fine Arts Collection*. Pp. 9-47. Phoenix, AZ: The Heard Museum.

   1976b   Spanish-American and Navajo Weaving, 1600 to Now. In *Collected Papers in Honor of Margery Ferguson Lambert*. A. Schroeder, ed. Papers of the Archaeological Society of New Mexico 3:199-226.

   1977   Documentary Basis for Material Changes and Design Styles in Navajo Blanket Weaving. In *Ethnographic Textiles of the Western Hemisphere*, 1977 Proceedings of the Irene Emery Roundtable on Museum Textiles. Irene Emery and Patricia Fiske, eds. Pp. 420-440. Washington, D.C.: The Textile Museum.

   1979b   Rio Grande, Pueblo, and Navajo Weavers: Cross-Cultural Influence. In *Spanish Textile Tradition of New Mexico and Colorado*. Nora Fisher, ed. Pp. 29-36. Santa Fe, NM: Museum of International Folk Art and Museum of New Mexico Press.

   1981   Early Navajo Weaving. *Plateau* 52(4):2-9. Museum of Northern Arizona, Flagstaff, AZ.

   1984   *The Gift of Spiderwoman: Southwestern Textiles, The Navajo Tradition*. Philadelphia: The University Museum, University of Pennsylvania.

   n.d.   Blanket Weavers of the Southwest. Manuscript, in the files of the author.

PLATE 1 Navajo "child's blanket," circa 1847; collected by Colonel Randall near Veracruz, Mexico, during the Mexican War (UCM 39310). Photo by Joe Ben Wheat.

PLATE 2 Navajo manta, circa 1750-1850; a "blue borders" manta representing one of the earliest known types of Navajo weaving (UCM 27484). Photo by Martin Natvig.

PLATE 3 *Navajo sarape, 1870-71; perhaps woven for Thomas Ewing, a government agent in the Southwest during the early 1870s (UCM 28849).* Photo by Inga Calvin.

PLATE 4 *Navajo sarape, circa 1840-60; an excellent example of Classic Period weaving at its height (UCM 23487).* Photo by Martin Natvig.

PLATE 5 *Hopi woman's manta ("maiden's shawl"), circa 1900 (W/TxP-7).* Photo by Martin Natvig.

PLATE 6 *Navajo blanket, circa 1896; all yarns in this Hubbell-influenced pattern are silk (UCM 38168).* Photo by Ken Abbott.

PLATE 7 *Navajo wedge weave blanket, circa 1876-80; woven by a Navajo servant in a Hispanic household, San Luis Valley, Colorado (UCM 18088).* Photo by Martin Natvig.

PLATE 8 *Spanish Colonial blanket, circa 1875-85; Vallero star pattern (5/15/81 #5).* Photo by Martin Natvig.

PLATE 9 *Mexican Saltillo sarape, circa 1750 (UCM 39306).* Photo by Martin Natvig.

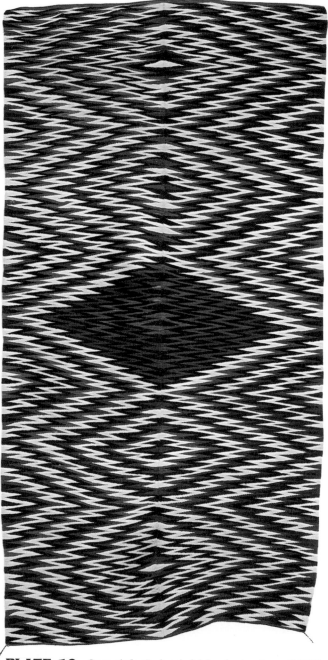

PLATE 10 *Spanish Colonial blanket, circa 1850 (Loan No. 326).* Photo by Martin Natvig.

COMPARISON OF SOUTHWESTERN TEXTILE TRAITS*

TRAITS	PUEBLO	NAVAJO	SPANISH-COLONIAL
STYLE			

DESIGNS	bands
	geometric motifs and
	   pictographic symbols
	horizontal dominance
	limited patterning
		bands
		terraced motifs
		horizontal dominance
		all-over patterning
		selective pictorial motifs
		   and scenes
			bands
			serrate motifs
			vertical dominance
			center-oriented patterning
			occasional stylized
			   pictorial motifs

CONSTRUCTION			
TYPE OF LOOM	upright string heddles batten hole/slot heddle (Zuni)	upright string heddles batten and comb	European floor loom suspended harnesses swinging beater shuttle
FORMAT	wider than long	wider than ong longer than wide	longer than wide
WEAVES	balanced twill weaves balanced plain weave weft-faced plain weave Hopi brocade weave (sashes) oblique interlacing (sashes) warp-float weave (belts)	tapestry weave weft-faced plain weave weft-faced twill weaves wedge weave warp-float weave (belts)	tapestry weave weft-faced plain weave balanced twill weaves (jerga)
CORNERS	loose knots	tightly worked knots augmented tassels	no special corner treatment

TRAITS	PUEBLO	NAVAJO	SPANISH-COLONIAL
CONSTRUCTION			
SELVAGES	continuous warp knotted warp ends rare (except Zuni) 3-strand twining with 2-ply cords on ends and sides (most common)	continuous warp knotted warp ends rare 2-strand twining with 3-ply cords on ends and sides (most common)	cut and knotted warp ends multiple side warps no twining
DETAILS	no lazy lines (Hopi) some lazy lines (Zuni)	lazy lines (common)	no lazy lines
AVERAGE WARP/ WEFT COUNT	5-8/20-35	7-12/25-60	5-7/25-35
MATERIALS			
FIBERS	handspun cotton commercial cotton string wool	wool commercial cotton string (warp) handspun cotton (rare)	wool cotton (less common) linen (rare)
YARNS	handspun commercial raveled	handspun (spindle) commercial raveled (common)	handspun (spindle and/or spinning wheel) commercial raveled (rare)
DYES			
DYESTUFFS	native, natural, aniline	native, natural, aniline	native, natural, aniline
CHARACTERISTIC COLORS	white, black, blue, and brown, predominate with red, green accents	widely varied	black, brown, blue, and white common; pastels (pinks, purples, oranges)

*Note: only the predominant types of traits and tendencies during the latter half of the nineteenth century are summarized here. Considerable variation exists in individual textiles.

Selections from the UCM Collection

The University of Colorado Museum currently curates approximately five hundred southwestern textiles and is an important resource for students, scholars, and others interested in the textile arts. All major periods and styles are represented and many pieces are documented, making this one of the ten top assemblages of southwestern weaving.

Although not all of the collection is well documented, the histories of some pieces are enlightening: the Randall sarape (39310 [Plate 1]), collected circa 1847, is the earliest known, documented Navajo wearing blanket. Blankets collected by Mary Loud Gay in the 1860s and 1870s (including 26341 [Fig. 11], 26383 [Fig. 12], and 29053), the Clinton blanket (23489 [Fig. 10]) collected in 1869-70, and two mantas (22493 and 22494) acquired by John Wesley Powell in the 1870s represent important keys to weaving in those decades. The Henrietta Grinnell Cole collection was made between 1895 and 1906 and contains every major kind of weaving that was current at that time. The wedge weave blanket (18088 [Plate 7]) woven by a Navajo servant in a Hispanic household provides clues to specific intercultural relations in the Southwest. Of particular aesthetic quality is the Heye sarape (23487 [Plate 4]), an example of quintessential classic style. Important for its materials is the Thomas Ewing sarape (28849 [Plate 3]) containing commercial yarns documented from 1870.

The following list provides basic information about a selection of one hundred and forty textiles from this collection. Those included are also part of the 1989-91 UCM Boulder exhibition, *Beyond the Loom: Keys to Understanding Early Southwestern Weaving*, in which three separate groups of textiles will be shown over three years on a one-year rotation. The final notation in each entry indicates the exhibition period during which the textile will be displayed (I for 1989, II for 1990, and III for 1991). A smaller selection of these textiles are illustrated by photographs in a traveling exhibition by the same name; these textiles are the same as these reproduced in this booklet.

The textiles are organized into twenty-six functional or stylistic categories, all of which are commonly used in the literature on southwestern weaving. The number at the beginning of each entry is the UCM registration number or the Wheat collection number. The basic format for the entries follows Kate Peck Kent's catalogue of the School of American Research Navajo textile collection (*Navajo Weaving: Three Centuries of Change*, 1985, Santa Fe, pp. 116-130). Provenance (prior collections) is listed in chronological order.

Selected textiles are illustrated in this book and are noted by a plate number for color or a figure number for black and white. Information about yarns, dyes and significant technical features is listed for these textiles; for those textiles not illustrated, brief notes about exceptional features are included. Measurements are given in inches and centimeters, with the length as measured along the warps always stated first. Direction of spin, number of plies in a yarn, and direction of final twist in a multiple-ply yarn are recorded; see the Glossary entry for definitions. Warp and weft counts are given as threads per inch (2.5 cm); when multiple strands of raveled yarns are used as one weft, each group of strands is counted as a single weft. Pueblo and Navajo selvage information refers to the number of cords twined and the makeup of each cord, and refers to both warp and weft selvages unless otherwise noted.

Observations made by Joe Ben Wheat follow the entries to which they pertain and are italicized. These are direct transcriptions from a series of tape-recorded conversations that Wheat had with graduate students Patricia Lawrence, Teresa Wilkins, and Jim Walton and with me during 1988.* In addition to providing more detail on the collection, such informal commentary is included here to introduce the reader to Wheat's approach in examining textiles and to illustrate points made earlier about the research process and its results.

The difficulty in selecting relatively few examples from the entire collection for publication should be evident. Although not all textiles

---

* I am indebted to Patricia Lawrence for making the recordings and for her careful transcription and organization of the lengthy results as part of a project funded by the Walker Van Riper Fund of the University of Colorado Museum. ALH

could be illustrated, we hope that the following descriptions at least whet your appetite for seeking out the "real things" in museum collections and wherever else you find them.

PUEBLO

Blankets

13983 Rio Grande (?) Pueblo, circa 1865-80; collected by homesteaders in southeastern Colorado around the time of the Civil War; gift of Katherine McIntyre. Uneven (2/1) diagonal and herringbone twill weaves. (I)

> *I think there's a good chance that this is a blanket from the Rio Grande Pueblos for a variety of reasons. Even though the selvage (two 3-ply cords) tends to suggest that it's a Navajo selvage, we don't know where the Navajo learned to make a selvage like that. The corners are loose, not the tightly tied corner that you get in Navajo weaving. This red, so rare in Navajo weaving that it's almost nonexistent, and the mahogany or cafe au lait color are Rio Grande or Spanish colonial dyes. They were not available out in the reservation country. The piece probably dates around 1880, possibly a little earlier than that. So anyway, everything about this blanket—the dyes, the weave itself, the ways the corners are finished, the early collection date—ties in with this being Pueblo rather than Navajo. Yes, I think it's an exciting piece.*

26338 Hopi, circa 1900; gift of Dorothy Odland and Carol Ann Mackay. (III)

26340 Zuni, circa 1870-90; gift of Mr. and Mrs. Jonathan Holstein and Mr. and Mrs. Philip Holstein, Jr. Includes natural grey wool characteristic of Zuni weaving and a coarse z-spun raveled red yarn. (II)

> *This is a Zuni blanket with raveled yarn for home use. There are several characteristics of Zuni here. There's no twined weft selvage. The warp selvage cord was tucked into the corner instead of being tied off—the Zunis are the only ones I know that do that. Zunis were still using raveled yarn as late as the 1890s. The raveled is very coarse, late, in singles and doubled. And*

finally the clincher is this grey wool. This is not a combed grey—this is a natural grey wool of Zuni sheep. I've never seen this particular wool except from Zuni.

26845 Zuni, circa 1870; gift of William Ackard. (III)

This is a variation on a "Moki" pattern. It's the alternation of the indigo blue and the dark brown [bands] that marks the pattern. In one end the blue is a lot darker than the other, which I find interesting. This was probably used as a bed blanket or utility blanket. It is pre-1875 because of the [commercial] 3-ply warp.

Hopi Plaid Shoulder Blanket

23576 Hopi "bachelor's" blanket, circa 1900; museum exchange. (II)

Hopi White Cotton Wedding Mantas

W/TxP-31 Wedding robe, circa 1880; ex coll. J.L. Hubbell, Wheat collection. Includes handspun and commercial cotton yarns. (I)

30332 Wedding robe (contained in reed suitcase), circa 1950; part of complete wedding outfit of Myrtle Tootsie, woven by her husband's family; Wheat collection. Includes handspun and commercial cotton yarns. (I)

White Mantas With Red and Blue Borders

W/TxP-7 Hopi, circa 1900; purchased at Keam's Canyon Trading Post, AZ; Wheat collection. 39" x 49" (100 x 123 cm). Warp: commercial cotton string, natural white, 22/inch. Wefts: handspun cotton, z, natural white, 16-40/inch; commercial wool, 4-ply split in two, z, paired, synthetic red and black. Selvage cords: handspun wool, 3 z, black. (I). Plate 5.

I bought this at Keams Canyon. It had been brought in by a Hopi. It's about the earliest one I have ever seen for sale under such circumstances.

9229 Hopi, circa 1900-20; gift of John Byrum. Includes handspun cotton and split commercial wool yarn. (II)

Figure 5. Acoma manta, circa 1850-60 (UCM 10342). Photo by Martin Natvig.

Black Wool Mantas, Embroidered

W/TxP-22 Zuni, circa 1875-80; Wheat collection. Includes small amount of commercial 3-ply yarn with synthetic dye. (II)

10342 Acoma, circa 1850-60; museum exchange. 43" x 61" (108 x 155 cm). Diagonal twill and plain weave, split stitch embroidery. Warp: handspun churro wool, z, natural brown-black, 18/inch. Weft: handspun churro wool, z, natural brown-black and indigo blue. Embroidery: raveled wool, 2z-S, lac red; commercial Saxony, 3z-S, red. Selvage cords: handspun wool, 3 2z-S, indigo blue. (I). Figure 5.

> There are only about 35 or 40 of these mantas known that have survived. This type disappeared by about 1855 or 1860. Most of the ones from Acoma have this type of design. The dye on this raveled red is consistently lac. The cloth that was being raveled is different than the cloth that was being used as a weft strand in Navajo weaving. The embroidery is typical of Pueblo embroi-

dery, which is apparently not very widely practiced anywhere else in the world. There's another interesting thing about these—when you're doing embroidery it's very difficult to embroider on a diagonal twill weave because you can't count. So, in these pieces they normally wove a diagonal center, and both ends are a balanced plain weave, so the embroidery could be counted.

Black Wool Manta Dresses

W/TxP-5 Zuni, circa 1870-80; purchased from Rex Arrowsmith, Wheat collection. (I)

This is a standard type of dress. It embodies all of the standard techniques of the dresses that postdate 1875. At the ends you have a selvage which is usually three 2-ply cords. This is an example of good wool—well spun—and really well-woven. This person really knew how to spin and weave. If you don't have fine threads, you can't weave well.

39335 Zuni, circa 1900; gift of H. Medill Sarkisian. (III)

We know that at Zuni in recent times, that is since the late 1880s, the women have been weavers. But the men know how to weave too. Does this mean that the women have taken this over for the last 150 years? There are a lot of questions that we need to answer. So far as I know the documents are either totally misleading or quiet on the subject.

Sashes With Ends Patterned by "Hopi Brocade"

20935 Circa 1875-1900; gift of Muriel Sibell Wolle. All wool, including 4-ply Germantown yarn. (III)

20983 Circa 1930s; gift of Muriel Sibell Wolle. 83" x 9½" (211 x 24 cm). Plain weave with extra weft wrapping. Warp: commercial cotton string, z, natural white. Weft: handspun wool, z, natural white. Weft-wrapping: 4-ply commercial wool, green, black, purple. (I). Figure 6.

26741 Circa 1880-1900; gift of Muriel Sibell Wolle. (II)

Figure 6. Hopi brocaded sash, circa 1930s (UCM 20983). Photo by Ken Abbott.

26825 Circa 1875-1900; Wheat collection. All wool, including 4-ply Germantown yarn. (II)

39334 Circa 1930s; gift of the Graham Foundation. (III)

W/TxP-12 Circa 1850-75; ex coll. Charles Eagle Plume, Wheat collection. Includes only wool yarns (handspun, raveled, and 3-ply). (I)

> *This is the only one of these sashes I have ever seen with raveled yarn.*

Fringed White Cotton Sashes

20978 Circa 1900, gift of Muriel Sibell Wolle. Handspun cotton. (III)

26373 Rio Grande Pueblo or Hopi, circa 1880-1900; purchased from Rex Arrowsmith, Wheat collection. Includes handspun cotton with commercial cotton repairs. (III)

26740 Circa 1870-80; gift of Muriel Sibell Wolle. Handspun cotton. (II)

30334 (Contained in reed suitcase) circa 1950; part of complete wedding outfit of Myrtle Tootsie, made by her husband's family; Wheat collection. Commercial cotton. (I)

L-240-3 Circa 1875-1900; Wheat collection. Handspun cotton. (I-III)

Belts, Garters, and Hair Ties

9232b Belt; gift of John Byrum. (II)

20984 Belt, Hopi; gift of Muriel Sibell Wolle. (II)

20985 Belt, Pueblo but Navajo style; gift of Muriel Sibell Wolle. (III)

26756 Belt, Hopi, circa 1930; gift of Muriel Sibell Wolle. (III)

26823 Belt, Hopi; Wheat collection. (I)

26824 Belt, Santa Ana Pueblo; Wheat collection. (I)

Other Garments

10343 Hopi blue wool shirt; museum exchange. (II)

28698 Zuni breech cloth, circa 1875; gift of Mr. and Mrs. Jonathan Holstein and Mr. and Mrs. Philip Holstein, Jr. (I)

30337 Crocheted leggings, Tewa pueblo (probably San Juan Pueblo), circa 1930; Wheat collection. Commercial cotton yarn. (II)

NAVAJO

We know pretty well that the Navajo learned to weave sometime in the late 1600s. And almost certainly they learned from the Pueblos. It would have been far more convenient for them to learn from some of the upper Rio Grande Pueblos—they were closest—[otherwise] they would have had to go all the way over to Zuni to get a teacher. But there are so many unknowns—what I'm saying is that we don't really know who taught the Navajo to weave. We know that they were Pueblo, and that's about all we do know. The reason we know that, of course, is because they adopted the Pueblo loom, the Pueblo spinning techniques, and the first garments they wove were typical Pueblo-like garments with their own modifications.

Women's Shoulder Blankets

10859 Terraced zigzags, circa 1870-80; ex coll. Earl Morris, gift of Lucille Morris. (I)

18080 "Diamond stripe" pattern, circa 1865-70; ex coll. William Neumiller, museum purchase. (II)

25077 Meander pattern, circa 1870s; gift of Dr. Charles M. Bogert. (III)

39228 Terraced diamonds and Spider Woman's crosses, circa 1890-1900; gift of the Graham Foundation. Includes 4-ply Germantown yarn. (III)

*This is a late copy of a woman's pattern blanket. It was proba-
bly woven at Hubbell's Trading Post. [This identification is made
for] two reasons: Hubbell commissioned a lot of these using [4-
ply] Germantown yarn, and in lots of these blankets there was
purple instead of blue. He very frequently [had weavers use]
Spider Woman crosses. This is really a combination of things.
It's very typical of what was going on in the late 1800s.*

Women's Mantas

L-172 Gift of the Graham Foundation. (III)

22493 Meander pattern, circa 1865-70; ex coll. John Wesley Powell,
gift of Mrs. Joseph P. Graves. (I)

*The first two mantas we got were a result of hearing a rumor
that a lady who lived in the mountains west of Denver was a
niece or daughter of John Wesley Powell and had some pieces
that she was trying to find a permanent home for. It took me
several weeks to chase her down. It turned out that she was the
great-niece of Powell and she had several things that he had
collected in 1870.*

22494 "Diamond stripe" pattern, circa 1865-70; ex coll. John Wesley
Powell, gift of Mrs. Joseph P. Graves. (II)

*The red yarn is an early 3-ply Germantown; there is some rav-
eled red too; the pink center is combed pink; the green and blue
are handspun. This was collected in 1870 when they would
have had the 3-ply early Germantown [that] had been issued to
them for several years. They were still getting it as part of
government issue up until 1878. Also bayeta was issued to
them during some of those years. This is a design that came in
with Saltillo [influences] as a diagonal rhomboid stripe, sometimes called a diamond stripe. The diamond stripe comes in
during the early 1860s.*

26385 Spider Woman's cross variant, circa 1865-75; museum purchase. 42" x 57" (107 x 145 cm). Diagonal and diamond twill tapestry
weaves. Warp: handspun wool, z, white, 16/inch. Weft: raveled wool,
z, red, 74-88/inch; handspun wool, z, indigo blue, 28/inch. Selvage
cords: commercial wool, 3 3z-S, red. (I). Figure 7.

Figure 7. Navajo manta, circa 1865-75 (UCM 26385). Photo by Martin Natvig.

This is the type that led me to call the category "fancy mantas." A number of Navajo mantas have been collected at Zuni and at Acoma but every time we were able to trace one back it turns out to be Navajo. Pueblos bought tremendous quantities of Navajo weaving. This one happens to be more intact than almost any other one I've seen. Most of these were really worn quite a bit.

27484 "Blue borders" manta, circa 1750-1850; gift of Joe Ben Wheat. 36" x 53" (91 x 134 cm). Balanced diagonal and diamond twill weaves. Warp: handspun wool, z, natural browns, 20/inch. Weft: handspun wool, z, natural browns and indigo blue, 27/inch. Selvage cords: warp, handspun wool, 2 2z-S, brown; weft, handspun wool, 3 2z-S, brown. (I). Plate 2.

One of the earliest types of Navajo weaving, resembling most closely the Pueblo prototype, except for the presence of lazy lines. Remember that these things were one of the first things that the Navajo made when they learned to weave. [A] very early [piece], the blue-borders is an open twill, just like the Pueblo. Navajos began moving away from the open twill sometime before 1750. The surprising thing to me is how quickly they began to adapt the [traits] which specifically are credited to the Navajo later on [for instance, the Navajo weft-faced twills and their 2-strand 3-ply selvage system]. By 1785 these were being replaced with the two-piece dress with red borders.

35667 Terraced diamonds, circa 1870; gift of Dorothy Goodwin. (II)

36564 Crosses, circa 1885-90; gift of the Graham Foundation. (III)

39212 Terraced zigzags, gift of Kenneth Siebel. (III)

44439 Gift of Dorothy Goodwin. (I)

Women's Two-Piece Dresses

10337 Spider Woman's crosses and terraced triangles, circa 1840-60; museum exchange. 45" x 35" (114 x 88 cm). Tapestry weave, interlocking joins. Warp: handspun wool, z, natural white, 17/inch. Weft: handspun wool, z, natural black, 80/inch; handspun wool, z, blue-black, 68/inch; raveled wool, s, cochineal red, 60 pairs/inch. Selvage cords: handspun wool, 2 3z-S, indigo blue. (II). Figure 8.

This was collected by Eric [Frederic] Douglas' father sometime before the turn of the century [Douglas was the renowned curator of the Denver Art Museum's Native Arts Department for many years]. This was the first dress we had in our collection and a superb piece of weaving. This [yarn] has been tested; it is cochineal.

19514 Spider Woman's cross variations and terraced triangles, circa 1870; gift of Elizabeth Roberts. (I)

19515 Terraced diamonds, circa 1840-60; gift of Elizabeth Roberts. (I)

26843 Terraced zigzags, circa 1875; gift of William Ackard. (II)

Figure 8. Navajo dress, circa 1840-60 (UCM 10337). Photo by Martin Natvig.

Figure 9. Navajo man wearing a chief style blanket. Archives of the University of Colorado Museum.

35666 Terraced triangles and diamonds, circa 1865-70; gift of Dorothy Goodwin. Includes early handspun aniline dyed red wool yarn. (III)

Chief Blankets

13143 Third phase, circa 1875-79; gift of John Hough. (II)

18063 Third phase, circa 1870; ex coll. Earl Morris, gift of Lucille Morris. (I)

> *The blanket was acquired by Earl sometime in the 1920s, but he was able to trace it back to 1870 when it was woven or collected. Earl was in the business of selling textiles from at least as early as 1915. There are a number of letters, particularly from people in St. Louis, buying textiles from Earl. He is the one who got [Gilbert] Maxwell started; a lot of the pieces at [the Maxwell Museum of] the University of New Mexico in Albuquerque had been part of Earl's collection. Earl kept six pieces which he used as lecture pieces—this is one of those. It's a perfectly classic so-called phase III chief blanket. They just don't come any more classic than this. The standard layout [is] of a full diamond in the center, half-diamonds at the ends and quarter diamonds at the corners. The red is a raveled yarn.*

26847 Third phase, circa 1880-85; gift of Mr. and Mrs. Victor Walker. (III)

33358 Second phase, circa 1860-65; gift of Edgar O. Smith. 55" x 68" (145 x 173 cm). Tapestry weave, interlocking joins. Warp: handspun wool, z, natural white, 4-10/inch. Weft: handspun wool, z, white, brown, blue, z, 44-54/inch; raveled wool, s, lac red, 68 groups/inch; raveled wool, z, cochineal red, 80-96 groups/inch. Selvage cords: handspun wool, 2 3z-S, indigo blue. (I)

> *This is a variation of the second phase chief blanket—a man's shoulder blanket, probably close to 1860. The standard design is blue stripes interrupted with red [rectangles], making a 12-spot pattern. Here, nested or concentric rectangles of blue and red occupy the same positions as [the plain rectangles normally would].*

39337 Second phase; gift of H. Medill Sarkisian. (II)

Sash Belts

9232a Gift of John Byrum. (I)

20986 Gift of Muriel Sibell Wolle. (III)

26358 Circa 1865; ex coll. LTC Inman; gift of Mr. and Mrs. Jonathan Holstein and Mr. and Mrs. Philip Holstein, Jr. Includes lac-dyed raveled yarn; one of two earliest known documented belts. (I)

26359 Circa 1865; ex coll. LTC Inman; gift of Mr. and Mrs. Jonathan Holstein and Mr. and Mrs. Philip Holstein, Jr. Includes cochineal-dyed 3-ply commercial Saxony yarn; one of two earliest known documented belts. (II)

26619 Gift of Dr. Isabel Bittinger. (II)

W/TxN-51 Wheat collection. (III)

Classic and Late Classic Period Blankets (Sarapes)

18058 Child's late classic sarape, compound bands with meander pattern, circa 1865-75; ex coll. Earl Morris, gift of Lucille Morris. (III)

> *This is an excellent piece for showing materials because you've got just about every material that was available to them in the late 1860s, going from the raveled and early 3-ply Germantown to the handspun. The orange and green are aniline and the red 3-ply yarn is cochineal dyed. The meander pattern appears in basketry and weaving in the early 1860s, along with Spider Woman's crosses, plain crosses, stacked triangles, and serrate diamonds with very tiny stepped edges. We don't know whether it's earlier in basketry or in weaving [nor] where it came from. 1862 is the earliest [meander in weaving] that I've recorded.*

18062 Child's late classic sarape, compound bands, circa 1870-80; ex coll. Earl Morris, gift of Lucille Morris. (II)

23487 Classic sarape, terraced pattern, circa 1840-60; bought in New York second hand shop in 1911, ex coll. George Heye, ex coll. Clay Lockett, ex. coll. Denver Art Museum, museum exchange. 76" x 50" (193 x 127 cm). Tapestry weave, interlocking joins. Warp: handspun wool, z, natural white, 15/inch. Weft: handspun wool, z, natural white, indigo blue, 47/inch; raveled wool, s, lac red, 56 groups/inch. Selvage cords: handspun wool, 2 3z-S, indigo blue. (I). Plate 4.

I would guess that sometime before 1840 this piece came across the Santa Fe Trail going back east. It turned up in a second hand shop in New York City about 1911 and was bought by George Heye who was the founder of the Museum of the American Indian. Sometime during the 1930s the piece was traded to a trader at Hopi. In Heye's catalogue it is described as a Saltillo sarape. It's one of the five best blankets in existence, for this time period. This is the piece that really tipped me off to the fact that the negative space in blanket design is just as important as the positive space. In particular this is where I began to realize that the zigzags are simply the spaces between opposed, offset, terraced triangles. Most of these early sarapes have a red background—virtually everything is weighted toward the red and blue. In many of the early pieces you've got interpenetration of the design panels; that is, the designs are not bound by straight lines and they interfigure or intermesh. Later everything is very neatly laid out in panels.

23489 (13273) Late classic sarape, terraced diamond network, circa 1869-70; made for Major William Clinton, superintendent of Indian Affairs in New Mexico from 1869 to 1870, gift of Mrs. Ellen Gary McKay. 71" x 51" (181 x 131 cm). Tapestry weave, interlocking joins. Warp: handspun wool, z, natural white, tan, brown, 12/inch. Weft: handspun wool, natural white, indigo blue, z, 50-60/inch; raveled wool, cochineal red, z, 42/inch. Selvage cords: handspun wool, 2 3z-S, indigo blue. (II). Figure 10.

This is very characteristic of the blankets being made at the end of the 1860s—the design, the layout, the corners, and the use of the raveled material. This is quite a different raveled material than was used earlier; this is much coarser. This is probably the best example of the so-called broken stripe background of any blanket I've ever seen, very characteristic of the period from

Figure 10. Navajo sarape, circa 1868-70 (UCM 23489). Photo by Martin Natvig.

about 1865 through the 1870s. William Clinton was superinten-
dent of Indian affairs in New Mexico from early 1869 to 1870,
and it was Clinton who, at the end of Bosque Redondo, pur-
chased the sheep which were delivered to the Navajo. Family
history has it that [this blanket] was made especially for him.

26341 Late classic sarape, terraced and meander patterns, circa
1860-63; collected before 1863 by Mary Loud Gay, gift of Dr. Isabel
Bittinger. 59" x 43" (148 x 108 cm). Tapestry weave, interlocking
joins. Warp: handspun wool, z, natural white, 16/inch. Weft: commercial Saxony wool, 3z-S, cochineal red, 64/inch; handspun wool, natural white, indigo blue, z, 64/inch. Selvage cords: handspun wool, 2
3z-S, indigo blue. (II-III). Figure 11.

This is one of the real examples of true Saxony, as opposed to
the early Germantown you commonly see referred to as Sax-
ony. This is three-ply, cochineal-dyed, very fine yarn. The blan-
ket was collected by a lady from Massachusetts who came out
in 1861 to stay with her relatives in the Southwest. At the be-
ginning of the Civil War in 1863 she went back home and while
she was there one of her hobbies was to collect Navajo textiles
right off the back of the owner when she could. Family history
says that she would trade [commercial] blankets and other
kinds of things to the Indians for these. It's extremely rare to
find a border enclosing early rugs. Normally borders don't
come in until 1880, and they become prevalent by 1890, but
there are maybe a half dozen earlier pieces known that have
borders and this is one of them.

Most blankets of the time period were slightly larger than this
[59" x 43"], but they did weave blankets to size for the people
who were going to wear them. Most of the blankets that the
childen wore, at least if you could judge by photographs at
Bosque Redondo and so forth, were this large or larger. The
child's blanket is a blanket that doesn't really come in until after
Bosque Redondo, when the Navajo went to the reservation, and
I think it has more to do with the commercial trend than the
child's wearing apparel. From 1870 on, the Navajo began to
weave more and more for sale to Anglos. Before they had wo-
ven for themselves and for people who actually wore Navajo
blankets as outer garments or dresses. Now they were selling to

Figure 11. Navajo sarape, circa 1860-63 (UCM 26341). Photo by Martin Natvig.

people who wanted to take them home as a souvenir of the Old West. A lot of things were made in smaller sizes because they were a lot faster to make and they were the type of thing that buyers could afford—a full size sarape would pose something of a problem.

26620 Child's sarape, terraced pattern, circa 1860-63; collected before 1863 by Mary Loud Gay, gift of Dr. Isabel Bittinger (I)

This is the beginning of the so-called child's blanket. They didn't start coming in until after the Civil War, after Bosque Redondo. The reason they started I think is because they're a lot faster to make than a full size sarape, they take less materials— you can make three of those with [the materials needed for] one full size sarape, and these would sell to the soldiers and the officers and to the first people who were coming into the Southwest after the Civil War to set up businesses and so on. They wanted something relatively cheap that they could take back home as a souvenir. Far more of these than full size blankets were taken back east. Another thing that you get in the same category are very fancy little saddle throws.

28849 Sarape, terraced and meander patterns, 1870-71; perhaps woven for Thomas Ewing ("T.E." initials in center) who was a government agent in the Southwest, collected by Mary Loud Gay, gift of Donnelley Erdman. 64" x 53" (162 x 135 cm). Tapestry weave, interlocking joins. Warp: 4-ply commercial cotton string, natural white, 11/inch. Weft: 3-ply Germantown yarn, 3z-S, dark blue, orange, red, white, light blue, yellow-orange, green, 52/inch. Selvage cords: 3-ply Germantown yarn, 3z-S, faded purple. (I). Plate 3.

Fortunately we have records of the Germantown [yarn] that was issued to the Navajo for most years in the U.S National Archives, in the letters received and sent from the Commissioner of Indian Affairs to various agents in the field. Every year the agents in the field would draw up a list of requirements for the Indians under their control or protection, then things would be purchased and sent out, usually in the fall. Those records are fairly complete. This blanket happens to have every single color of yarn that was issued in 1870—bought in 1870 but probably issued very late in 1870 so it was probably woven after that. Some of these colors were never issued before or since and so that's why we can be fairly certain that the date is 1870 or 1871.

30346 Child's late classic sarape, terraced and serrate patterns, circa 1870; Wheat collection. Includes raveled yarn. (III)

Because of the use of both terraced and serrate figures, this is a good so-called transitional piece. Like many transitional pieces, it has a wide variety of materials, from two different kinds of raveled material—the orange-red is coarse and the crimson is much finer, and there's a 4-ply and handspun as well.

39310 "Randall sarape" child's blanket, circa 1847; museum purchase. 48" x 31" (121 x 78 cm). Tapestry weave, interlocking joins. Warp: handspun wool, z, natural white, 10-11/inch. Weft: handspun wool, z, natural white, indigo blue, vegetal yellow, 44/inch; raveled wool, s and z, lac and cochineal reds, 68 pairs/inch. Selvage cords: handspun wool, 2 3z-S, indigo blue. (I). Plate 1.

This piece was brought to my attention by Fred Boschan who found it in an antique store in Pennsylvania. He had been given the family story by the dealer who got it from descendants of the original collector. Randall was a medical doctor and officer in the U.S. Army during the Mexican War in 1847. The family's history said that he'd collected this blanket while stationed in Veracruz. At the time when Fred contacted me, I happened to be in Washington working in the national archives, so I checked the military records and found out, indeed, that Randall had been there in 1847. During his entire military career he had never been closer to the Southwest than Oklahoma and Mexico. You don't always find a family story confirmed so neatly as this one.

Transition Period Blankets (Sarapes) and Rugs

10462 Sarape, banded, circa 1870-90; gift of Helen Borland. (II)

This is a typical, late aniline-dyed, utility blanket; it's not a flashy blanket. The use of indigo still continued until roughly 1900, but everything else here is aniline. It's just a simple striped blanket in which maroon, white, and blue stripes alternate with maroon, yellow, and black stripes. The red back-

ground is unusual in a piece like this; very typically this would have a white background with the tricolored stripes.

21078 Germantown eye dazzler, circa 1890; museum purchase. (II)

26383 Child's sarape, serrate pattern with terraced elements, circa 1875; ex coll. Mary Loud Gay, gift of Dr. Isabel Bittinger. 47" x 34" (119 x 86 cm). Tapestry weave, interlocking and diagonal joins. Warp: handspun wool, z, natural white, 14/inch. Weft: commercial wool, 3z-S and 4z-S, aniline red, yellow, blue, light green, 40/inch. Selvage cords: warp, commercial wool, 2 3(3z-S)Z, red; weft, commercial wool, 2 2(3z-S)Z, red. (I). Figure 12.

After we analyzed this I realized not all the blankets [collected by Mary Loud Gay] predated 1863. I began to probe the donor as to where all these things came from and she said that after her grandmother came home, her relatives in the Southwest kept sending her pieces. This is one of the early examples in which Saltillo designs were being used—essentially a serrate pattern. This comb-like pattern [however] is an early [Navajo] basketry design, but it doesn't come in until after the early 1860s. These little checkerboard diamonds are another form that came in during the 1860s. [The year] 1875 was the time when 4-ply replaced 3-ply so you've got a very tight lock on when this one was woven.

26753 Sarape, terraced zigzags, circa 1875-85; ex coll. John Byrum, gift of Muriel Sibell Wolle. (I)

This is 4-ply Germantown all the way through, with handspun white and two different indigo blues. This is one of the earlier pieces where the influence of the vertical alignment of Saltillo weaving appears in Navajo. This is probably 1875-85 based on materials and design style. They were still using a lot of crosses. Crosses are certainly far more common in the 1870s than they were in any time in the late 1880s. And the combination of zigzagged edges and stepped edges [in the motifs] means it's truly a transitional blanket.

29053 Child's sarape, terraced and serrate patterns, circa 1875; ex coll. Mary Loud Gay, gift of Dr. Isabel Bittinger. (II)

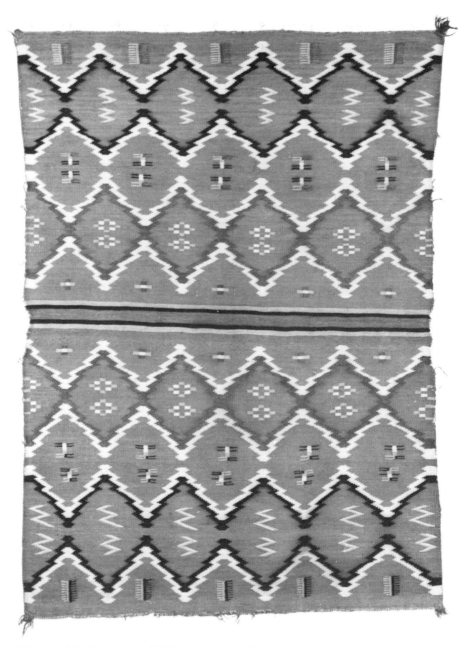

Figure 12. Navajo "child's" sarape, circa 1875 (UCM 26383). Photo by Martin Natvig.

All the commercial yarns in this are 4-ply, aniline-dyed. This pink is a color that you get a lot in the 1870s. One [motif] has full serrate edges. Combined with the checkerboard of alternating colors and the little vertical zigzags—this is a marvelous transitional piece [that shows] some of the figures that were coming in at that time.

33317 Child's blanket, terraced Hubbell pattern (identical to 38168), circa 1896; gift of Dorothy Goodwin (III)

This and 33317 were both made after a painting done about 1896. The donor's aunt collected this piece, probably at Hubbell's, when she was in the Southwest from 1895 to 1906. The two earliest examples of silk in Navajo blankets are both 3-ply commercial yarn. This one is floss silk and there are at least three and probably four of these blankets that were made at the same time. Hubbell brought in the silk and had two of them made for his daughters. Then C.N. Cotton, who was his partner for a while wanted one. This particular one was seen by a collector named Rohr from Milwaukee who bought it from Hubbell in 1896. When his whole collection was for sale, I decided to buy this one.

36560 Eye-dazzler blanket, circa 1885; gift of the Graham Foundation. 77" x 56" (196 x 141 cm). Tapestry weave, interlocking and diagonal joins. Warp: commercial cotton string, natural white, 8/inch. Weft: 4-ply Germantown yarn, red, black, purple, maroon, teal, white, light green, 60/inch; raveled wool, s, lac red. (I). Figure 13.

The raveled yarn in this piece is dyed with lac so this is something that [the weaver might have] had in a foot locker or around for a long time. She [raveled] an old piece of cloth that was hanging around. Everything else is 4-ply.

38168 Silk child's blanket, terraced Hubbell pattern (identical to 33317), circa 1896; Wheat collection. (III). Plate 6.

39227 Blanket, outlined serrate pattern with comb elements, circa 1875-85; gift of the Graham Foundation. (I)

The interesting thing about this is that it's a serrate outline pattern done in handspun. Most of the serrate outline patterns were

Figure 13. Navajo eye dazzler, circa 1885 (UCM 36560). Photo by Martin Natvig.

done in Germantown. It's the combination of the dyes and the handspun that makes it a superior piece, I think. The use of greens and yellows against a red ground and, of course, the use of indigo blue—it's just a super piece for the time period 1875-85.

39330 Eye-dazzler blanket/rug with meander border, circa 1900; gift of Michael and Susan McCabe. Includes late Germantown yarns. (II)

W/TxN-7 Germantown eye dazzler, 1887; collected in 1887 by R. J. Walker, Wheat collection. (III)

This was collected by my cousin's grandfather. There are two blankets from that time period that he collected. It's all 4-ply Germantown. It's of slightly odd proportions in that it is wider than a blanket this long would normally be. Clearly it's aniline dye—[the color has] bled in a few places.

Diyugi

Most diyugis were made to be worn and most of them got worn out and thrown away, which is the reason you find very few. For every fine sarape there were probably twenty diyugis woven and simply used up.

13654 Compound bands, circa 1865-78; given to W.S. Home by Chief Ouray in 1878-79, gift of J.M. Home. 67" x 54" (169 x 138 cm). Tapestry weave, diagonal joins; weft-faced plain weave. Warp: handspun wool, z, natural white, 6/inch. Weft: handspun *churro* wool, z, natural white and aniline dyed colors, 18/inch. Selvage cords: handspun wool, 2 3z-S, pink. (II)

18089 Serrate diamonds and zigzags, circa 1875-80; ex coll. Gerald Cassidy, gift of Hugo Rodeck. (III)

21074 Compound bands, circa 1870-80; museum purchase. Includes raveled and respun flannel. (III)

33993 Compound bands, circa 1870-80; Wheat collection. (III)

39304 Stacked triangles, circa 1890; gift of the Graham Foundation. (II)

Moki Pattern Blankets

In the "Moki pattern," the background consists of alternating brown and blue stripes. I have only seen one Moki with provenience from the Hopi—woven and collected about 1897. Al Whiting, who probably knew as much about Hopi weaving as anyone who ever lived, because he lived with them and worked with them as a weaving analyst, said he never saw a Moki pattern among the Hopi. Most of the attributions are simply based on the old word, Moki [another name for Hopi], rather than any real collection data.

23488 Compound bands with "diamond stripes," circa 1865-75; museum exchange. Includes commercial 3-ply yarn. (I)

The 3-ply yarn [in this] may have been called Saxony on the original analysis but that was before we knew a lot about it. Anything 3-ply in the early days was called Saxony. I'd call it early Germantown. This 3-ply pink-orange is almost certainly aniline. It is a very standard color alongside the red in early 3-ply pieces. The accompanying 3-ply red is cochineal but is certainly a lot coarser, less silky, yarn than true Saxony. This piece should date somewhere around 1870, give or take five years.

25124 Compound bands with "diamond stripes," circa 1875-85; museum purchase. (I)

26147 Compound bands with terraced diamonds and crosses, circa 1875; collected by Mary Loud Gay, gift of Dr. Isabel Bittinger. (I)

This is a very typical Navajo example of the so-called Moki pattern. The design is typical of that late Classic period in which the ends are laid out in a perfectly standard early Classic design of triangles. In the center, it has a row of diamonds with crosses in blue tipped with white. These are the crosses that came in during the early 1860s and by the 1870s they were a very standard, common type of cross design.

33359 Compound bands with "beading," 1860-65; gift of Eleanor Tulman-Hancock. Includes early 3-ply Germantown yarn. (III)

33990 Compound bands with "beading," circa 1850-70; Wheat collection. (II)

Wedge Weave Blankets

There are three varieties of wedge weave. Probably the most common one is the one in which [bands] of wedge weave [alternate] with panels of plain weave. Another variation is where very minute places of wedge weave are introduced into an otherwise plain tapestry weave. In the third category the wedge weave [is continuous] and the direction [of each diagonal band] is reversed so that it [makes an all-over diamond or zigzag pattern]. I think that the wedge weave technique may have been invented in the Rio Grande Valley rather than farther into the Navajo country, because many of the early ones I've seen tend to have more of the color cast of the Spanish American than anything else. There was a very short period of time when they were made—about 1875 to 1890. There probably never were more than a few hundred of these woven.

18088 Banded, circa 1876-80; woven by Guadalupe, a Navajo *criada* (servant) of the Dario Gallegos household in the San Luis Valley of southern Colorado, gift of Lauretta Bellamy. 71" x 50" (180 x 127 cm). Weft-faced plain weave and eccentric (wedge) weave. Warp: handspun wool, z, natural white, 6/inch. Weft: handspun wool, z, aniline dyed colors, natural white and grey, 14/inch. Selvages: warp, handspun wool, 2 3z-S, tan; weft, handspun wool, 2 2z-S, tan. (I). Plate 7.

This piece was woven by a Navajo lady named Guadalupe who was a slave in a Spanish household in the San Luis Valley and was given to us by the granddaughter of the man who owned the slave. He was one of the first settlers in the San Luis Valley who moved out from Costilla in northern New Mexico in 1859 and was running sheep up there. One of the interesting things about this piece is that it is still the old churro sheep wool and the dye colors are typical Spanish dye colors. This orange is synthetic dye that was invented and marketed in 1876 [Orange II] so this piece has to have been made after 1876, but probably not long after. Max Saltzman tested it.

22474 Diamond pattern, circa 1875-85; museum purchase. Includes 3-ply and 4-ply Germantown yarns. (II)

This is an example of the third category [continuous wedge weave]. Most of the wedge weaves were diyugis. You very rarely find a tightly woven wedge weave; for the most part they were very thick and fairly crude. This one is very tightly packed. Black is seldom used in Navajo weaving as a background color.

22475 Zigzag pattern, circa 1885; museum purchase. (III)

Pictorials

16034 Germantown blanket, serrate diamond network with crosses, bows and arrows, shovels, goats, horses, dragonflies, roadrunners, and chickens, circa 1875-1900; museum purchase. (III)

The use of curved lines is very unusual in southwestern weaving [although] they are common in European tapestry weaving. But if you notice, most of the bird figures are woven in place with curved lines—all of the feathers, the form of the body, and so on. There are some other curved elements, too—[such as] the bows. Some of the other figures are arrows, shovels, and a number of small crosses—these were all fairly common in the pictorials of the 1870s of which this is an example. [It was probably made around] 1875 or 1880.

21071 Diyugi, compound bands with cows(?), circa 1860; museum purchase. Tapestry weave, dovetailed joins. Warp: handspun wool, z, natural white, 4/inch. Weft: handspun wool, z, natural white, brown-black, combed gray, 18-24/inch; ravelel wool, s, lac + cochineal red, 4-6/inch. Selvage cords: handspun wool, 2 2z-S, white and brown. (I). Figure 14.

This is the only pictorial I've ever seen with raveled yarn.

26382 Blanket, banded, serrate diamonds and zigzags with cows and chickens, circa 1875; collected by Mary Loud Gay, gift of Dr. Isabel Bittinger. (II)

This piece is representative of a group with similar animals and layouts, some of which may have been woven by the same person. I've seen about four or five of these in other museums. I think that this is an example of something that caught the fancy

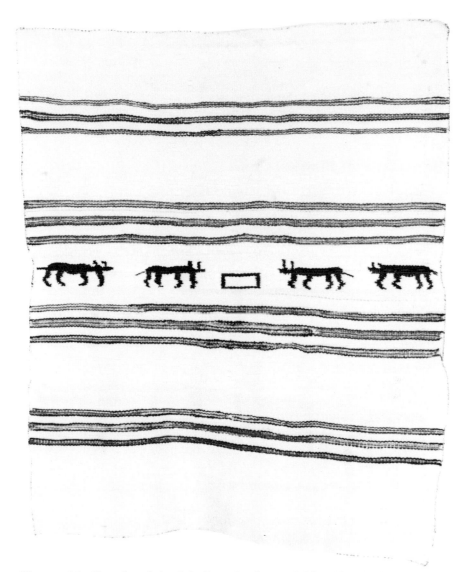

Figure 14. Navajo pictorial diyugi, circa 1860 (UCM 21071). Photo
by Martin Natvig.

of the buying public and was pursued with some vigor. This is basically all handspun except for the use of a little bit of 4-ply Germantown. It has the lavender of an early period. This had to be one that was sent to Mary Loud Gay after she left the Southwest because the aniline dyes and 4-ply yarns suggest the date of 1875, possibly a little later.

Germantown Blankets and Rugs

21080 Sarape, serrate diamonds, circa 1900; exhibited at St. Louis World's Fair in 1903, museum purchase. (III)

The principal line of interest in this blanket is the use of multiple serrate diamonds in a series of stacks with lots of color variation, symmetrical around the center. This was the piece the Wetherill brothers exhibited at the St. Louis World's Fair in 1906.

26846 Blanket, serrate diamonds, circa 1885; gift of William Ackard. (II)

This is a Navajo variation of Saltillo design. Once the idea of concentric diamonds was introduced, [the Navajos] did all sorts of variations on their own. In Saltillo, you wouldn't get a whole stack of [elements], you'd get one major one in the center.

Saddle Blankets, Covers, and Cinches

Saddle throws are very common, [and were often] collected and taken back East. They were easy to carry and colorful.

W/TxN-33 Tufted saddle cover, circa 1960; Wheat collection. (I)

This is representative of a type of tufted weave that was probably developed around 1875 to 1880. It was used basically for saddle throws [on top of the saddle] rather than for saddle blankets. The mohair, or angora, wool tufts are just laid [into the weave] at intervals, just worked right into the background.

18060 Double saddle blanket, banded with diagonal elements; ex coll. Earl Morris, gift of Lucille Morris. Weft-faced twill weave. (I)

This is a documented piece that shows several things. It was given as a wedding present in 1873. Earl Morris collected this from the family. This is all aniline with the possible exception of indigo in the blue and green. One other thing is the use of black wool for warp. Black wool was frequently used in the early days for warp in all kinds of weaving. They had a lot of black sheep and had to have some way to get rid of the wool. This was one of the ways that they could do that—simply spin it up and conceal it with the colored wefts. Sometimes you'll find it combed with white to make gray—"combed gray." Generally speaking, any time you see a blanket with a dark warp, it indicates a fairly early blanket.

18061 Saddle blanket, serrate pattern; ex coll. Earl Morris, gift of Lucille Morris. (I)

Saddle blankets didn't become popular until the late part of the [19th] century. I hear all these stories about saddles that went to Bosque Redondo on the Long Walk and there's really very little historical evidence to back that up. It looks like they were using sheepskin for saddle blankets and some kind of saddle that was far simpler.

22472 Saddle blanket, serrate pattern with meander border, circa 1875-80; museum purchase. (I)

This is a very small decorative cloth which could have been used as a saddle throw but may very well have been a forerunner of the later "runners." It is composed of 4-ply commercial Germantown yarn, plus some late raveled, a very fine material. It's this combination of materials that makes this an unusual piece. The design, a complex variety of meander, was current in the 1870s. The center design consists of stacked triangles with very fine comb-type edges.

35662 Saddle blanket; gift of Dorothy Goodwin. (I)

This is probably a saddle throw; it is about the right size for it.

13124 Double saddle blanket; gift of the Earl A. Mosley family. (II)

1983-43-171 Saddle blanket, terraced triangles, circa 1880-90; gift of Dorothy Goodwin. (II)

The lavender [color] in this is the old magenta [fuschin aniline dye] or some later derived formula. I expect this piece dates [from] 1880 to 1900. This lavender color was finally replaced by darker purples around 1890 or so, but much of the earlier purple had [a paler] cast.

1983-43-32 Saddle blanket, circa 1890-1900; gift of Dorothy Goodwin. (II)

This saddle throw has heavy fringe [made from uncut warps that extend beyond the weaving]. This is not a common thing. The weaver has utilized [a warp of] different colors to show up in the fringe.

26146 Saddle throw/cover, circa 1880-1900; Wheat collection. (II)

This is just a fancy little saddle throw, all Germantown with a comb pattern, vertical zigzags, heavy fringe, and heavy tassels. It would have been very dashing on a good looking horse and rider. This comb-type pattern doesn't really become prominent until about 1890 or so. Saddle blankets and throws are commonly wider than long.

26841 Double saddle blanket, comb-edged zigzags and diamonds, circa 1890; gift of William Ackard. (II)

This is a twill double saddle blanket with a vertical zigzag design. Twill adapts itself very well to this type of design. It's all handspun, all aniline dye with maroon, red, black, dark blue, green, orange, and some yellow, with cotton warp.

21081 Germantown twill saddle cover, diamond and block pattern, circa 1895-1900; museum purchase. (III)

This has a very fine twill and very complex pattern made possible by fine Germantown commercial yarns. Several [weft] passages use speckled yarns, which in general come in during the 1880s and persist up to about 1890-95. This little piece of weav-

ing was made by the Navajo wife of a trader somewhere over in the central Lukachukai area.

10336 Saddle blanket, vertical zigzags and quartered diamonds; museum exchange. (III)

This is a very fine little Germantown piece with a very typical Navajo use of a Saltillo pattern in which quartered diamonds are flanked by vertical zigzags and a [wide] combination of colors. Whether this was a double saddle blanket or wearing blanket (which its fineness might indicate) would be open to interpretation.

35660 Double saddle blanket, meander variant; gift of the Graham Foundation. (III)

39319 Saddle blanket, diamond twill weave; gift of the Graham Foundation. (III)

39301 Saddle blanket, diamonds, triangles and meanders, circa 1885; gift of the Graham Foundation. (III)

26148 Double saddle blanket, vertical zigzag pattern, circa 1900; gift of Dr. Isabel Bittinger. (III)

This is a saddle blanket or small rug—by this time sometimes you can't really tell the difference. It poses a real problem in terms of time because if this was in fact collected by Mary Loud Gay [the donor's grandmother] it had to be collected fairly early, yet it doesn't have the characteristics of a really early piece. All the dyes are aniline; the [texture of the spinning] and the wool [suggest] that it probably was [made] around Chinle around the turn of the century. I'm inclined to think that this probably came into the Bittinger family not through Mary Loud but some time later.

35663 Saddle cinch, serrate diamonds and stacked triangles, circa 1890; gift of Dorothy Goodwin. (III)

35665 Saddle cinch, zigzag, circa 1890; gift of Dorothy Goodwin. (II)

39320 Saddle cinch, diamond pattern; gift of Dorothy Goodwin. (I)

SPANISH COLONIAL (HISPANIC)

Saltillo Sarapes

Customarily in Saltillo [weaving] you get the use of very fine handspun 2-ply cotton warp, occasionally linen and very occasionally silk. Mostly it's very fine wool.

39306 Concentric serrate diamond with vertical zigzag background, circa 1750; gift of H. Medill Sarkisian. 99" x 53" (251 x 135 cm). Tapestry weave, diagonal and dovetailed joins. Warp: handspun cotton, natural white, 34/inch. Weft: handspun wool, natural white, red, blue, pink, 58/inch. (I). Plate 9.

39336 Concentric serrate diamond with lozenge patterned background, circa 1750; gift of H. Medill Sarkisian. (II)

Blankets

15991 Banded, circa 1865-75; gift of Katherine McIntyre. (III)

22479 Double-length blanket, compound bands, circa 1870-80; museum purchase (II)

25042 Banded, circa 1850-70; gift of Mr. and Mrs. David Raffelock. 84" x 51" (214 x 130 cm). Weft-faced plain weave. Warp: handspun wool, 2z-S, natural white, 6/inch. Weft: handspun wool, z, natural brown, white, indigo blue, 42/inch. Selvages: doubled outer warps. (I). Figure 15.

35669 Terraced diamond network; gift of the Graham Foundation. (III)

39323 Compound bands; gift of H. Medill Sarkisian. (II)

39325 Terraced diamonds; gift of the Graham Foundation. (II)

39462 Terraced vertical zigzags, circa 1870; gift of the Graham Foundation. (II)

39327 Banded; gift of the Graham Foundation. (III)

38189 Gift of the Graham Foundation. (III)

Figure 15. Spanish Colonial blanket, circa 1850-70 (UCM 25042).
Photo by Martin Natvig.

39461 Blanket half, concentric serrate diamonds, circa 1860; gift of the Graham Foundation. (III)

39296 Compound bands with serrate motifs, circa 1880s; gift of the Graham Foundation. (III)

5/15/81 #5 Vallero style, circa 1875-85; Wheat collection. 77" x 52" (196 x 131 cm). Tapestry weave, dovetailed joins; one piece woven on wide loom. Warp: handspun wool, z, natural white, 7-8/inch. Weft: handspun wool, z, tan, pale green, crimson, lavender, and pale yellow, 24/inch. Selvages: warp fringe, paired outer warps. (I). Plate 8.

W/TxC-5 Moki pattern patched with *jerga*, circa 1850-70; purchased from Elmer Shupe, Taos, NM, Wheat collection. (I)

W/TxC-4a Compound bands with terraced "diamond stripes," circa 1870; purchased from Elmer Shupe, Taos, NM, Wheat collection. (I)

W/TxC-3 Circa 1870; collected off of a wagon seat owned by a San Juan Pueblo Indian, ex coll. Jack Lambert, ex coll. Al Packard, Wheat collection. (I)

W/TxC-2 Terraced pattern showing Navajo influence, circa 1850; Wheat collection. 77" x 53" (197 x 135 cm). Tapestry weave, dovetailed joins; two pieces seamed at center. Warp: handspun wool, z, natural white, 6/inch. Weft: handspun wool, z, natural white, natural dark brown, indigo blue, 32/inch. Selvages: warp fringe, paired outer warps. (I). Figure 16.

> *This is a copy of a Navajo design certainly. These people were copying back and forth. The Spanish were making copies of Saltillo and Navajo blankets, and the Navajos every once in a while would make a copy of a Saltillo. The Navajo design elements are arranged in a style that was perfectly normal for Saltillo or Rio Grande with a center diamond and patterned corners. It's the use of the terraced triangles that shows the Navajo influence. Everything else about the blanket is perfectly typical Spanish.*

Jerga

26354 Diagonal twill weave, houndstooth check pattern, circa 1850; gift of Jack and Marjorie Lambert. (III)

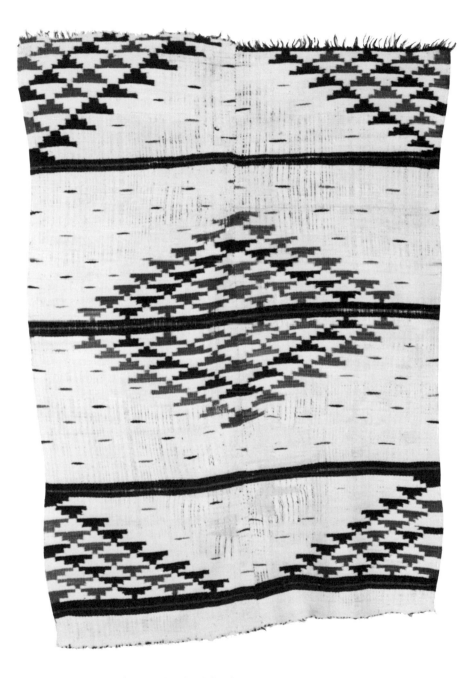

Figure 16. Spanish Colonial blanket, circa 1850 (W/TxC-2). Photo by Martin Natvig.

Glossary of Southwestern Weaving

The following definitions apply specifically to the collections of the University of Colorado Museum, and have also been used in the collection catalogues of the Navajo Tribal Museum, Arizona State Museum, and the Museum of Northern Arizona. These terms may have different meanings when used in other contexts. Comments by Joe Ben Wheat appear in italics.

Aniline dye *see* Dye

Augmented tassels Corner tassels in which additional yarn is inserted into the fabric's corners and looped through the fabric several times; each loop is left loose to form a decoration and to reinforce the corner's edges. Common on Navajo textiles. (See Plate 3 and Figure 8.)

Banded A design of horizontal (i.e., in the weft direction) elements, either of solid colors or with patterns running across each band; as opposed to striped, running in a vertical (warp-wise) direction. (See Plate 1.)

> **Compound or zoned bands** A design layout in which units of horizontal bands are regularly spaced and repeated with some regular rhythm; bands may be of solid colors or may have patterns within them. (See Figure 15.)

Bar A segment of a band, usually not extending from selvage to selvage. (See Figure 10.)

Batten A flat, broad stick used in Navajo and Pueblo weaving to open and maintain the weaving shed and, sometimes, to compact weft yarns into the weave. Usually several inches wide and a foot and a half long.

Bayeta A generic term for several types of trade cloth which was commonly raveled and re-used as weft in nineteenth century Navajo and some other textiles The term is Spanish, the English word being baize, but fabrics from Spain, England, elsewhere in Europe, the Near East, Mexico, New Mexico, and New England were obtained and raveled by the Navajos. Usually dyed red with cochineal, lac, a combination of the two, or with aniline dyes, but other natural and synthetic colors have also been reported.

Beading A small-scale woven pattern created by the alternation of two different colored wefts in a weft-faced fabric (or warps in a warp-faced fabric), resulting in small lines or blocks.

Blanket A rectangular fabric made in any of a variety of weaves and patterns, usually softly woven in order to drape around the body or to be used as bedding.

> **Chief blanket** A distinctive style of Navajo shoulder blanket and some rugs that are made wider than long. Two zones of wide black and white bands are separated by a series of narrower blue, black, and/or red bands along the ends and across the blanket's center, often with diamonds, rectangles, or other geometric motifs placed in three rows of three motifs each (see Nine-spot pattern). For ease of identification, chief blankets are divided into four phases, although the patterns overlap in time and continued in use during the late nineteenth and twentieth centuries. (See Figure 9.)
>
> > **First Phase (1800-1850)** Simple weft bands in black and white alternating with zones of dark blue and sometimes red.
> >
> > **Second Phase (1850-1870)** Bands still prominent, with 9 or 12 rectangles added as design elements. At first small, later rectangles are larger and often create gridlike effects.
> >
> > **Third Phase (1865-1875)** Rectangles modified into 9 small diamonds, which give way in later times to exploded diamond shapes that dominate the pattern.
> >
> > **Fourth Phase (1870-1900)** Increasingly elaborate shoulder blanket designs of the Transition Period. Sometimes the diamonds in such pieces are so large that the once dominant

black and white bands become background. Serrate patterns replace classic terraced designs. Elaborations such as pictorial motifs or continuous (edge to edge) motifs are sometimes woven into these blankets.

Child's blanket A small, sarape-style blanket. Recent study has suggested that many so-called child's blankets of the late nineteenth century may actually have been woven for use as trade items or souvenirs rather than for native children's use. (See Plate 1 and Figures 11 and 12.)

Diyugi Navajo word meaning "soft, fluffy blanket" at the turn of the century; used by historians for the coarse, handspun wearing blankets of everyday quality, generally longer than wide, with simple patterns and coloration. Currently used by Navajos as a generic term for any handwoven rug. (See Figure 14.)

Sarape (also spelled serape) A rectangular fabric woven longer (in the warp direction) than wide (in the weft direction), about six or seven feet long and three to four feet wide. Worn draped over the shoulders or around the body, it served as a primary outer garment and as a sleeping blanket for Mexicans and Southwesterners in the nineteenth century. (See Plates 1, 3, 4, and 9.)

Shoulder blanket A rectangular fabric that was worn draped over the shoulders or around the body.

Woman's blanket A rectangular, wider-than-long fabric, smaller than a man's blanket. Typical designs are similar to those of chief blankets, except that the bands are narrower and darker, with gray bands instead of white ones.

Blend Wool of several colors that has been carded together to produce a third color; most often, natural black-brown and natural white are combined to make a blended gray.

Bosque Redondo An alternative name for Fort Sumner, New Mexico, where the Navajo were held by the U.S. government from 1863 to 1868, in an effort to control and "civilize" them. Rounded up by Kit Carson and his men, the Navajos were taken on "The Long Walk" from their lands to the camp at Bosque Redondo, hundreds of miles away from their homes. Many people died, livestock were slaughtered, lands were lost—life changed dramatically for the Navajo at this time. The people were exposed to many new trade items and to very different lifestyles. Although some returned to northern Arizona after 1868, life was never the same. Bosque Redondo remains a symbol for this major turning point in Navajo life and culture.

Carding The process of cleaning and straightening wool in preparation for spinning by brushing the fibers with a pair of carders (flat brushes with wire teeth set closely in rows and held by handles attached at one end) or with a mechanized carding machine.

Chief blanket *see* Blanket

Child's blanket *see* Blanket

Chimayo A Spanish-American town in the Rio Grande Valley of New Mexico, where many weavers have made blankets, rugs, and runners on European-style floor looms for generations.

Churro wool *see* Wool

Classic Period, Classic style of Navajo weaving

> **Classic Period** (prior to 1865) This "traditional" phase is known for fine blankets, mantas, and other garments, woven for Navajo use and intertribal trade. Terraced tapestry patterns on dresses and blankets evolved from simple, right-angled basketry designs. The sarape-style blankets of the period are characterized by intense, densely integrated design schemes of terraced geometric elements, using a limited number of colors (natural white and brown, indigo blue, and raveled insect-dyed red). (See Plate 4.)

> **Late Classic Period** (circa 1865-1885) This early "transitional" period is marked by increasing influences from the outside. Many sarape-style blankets have patterns related to the terraced design schemes from the earlier Classic Period but are characterized by increased banding in patterned areas (i.e., less densely integrated pattern), and serrate motifs borrowed from Hispanic or Mexican weaving. Many different colors and types of yarns (especially 4-ply Germantown yarns, a number of raveled and raveled/respun materials, handspun wool, and so on) were combined.

Cochineal dye *see* Dye

Combed gray A gray wool yarn created by blending natural black and white wool fibers together.

Commercial yarn *see* Yarn

Compound bands *see* Banded

Continuous warp *see* Warp

Diamond stripe A band segmented diagonally into a series of rhombs or diamonds. (*See* Plate 6.)

Diyugi *see* Blanket

Double saddle blanket *see* Saddle blanket

Dovetailed joins *see* Tapestry weave under Weave

Dress
> **One-piece dress** Rectangular garment that is woven wider than long. It is worn folded in half, draped under one arm, with the upper corners being fastened over one shoulder, belted at the waist. Pueblo and the earliest Navajo dresses are of this style, in dark blue and brown-black wool twill weaves. Some Pueblo dresses have embroidered borders. Related to Manta.

> **Two-piece dress** Traditional garment worn by Navajo women in the nineteenth century, made of two identical, rectangular panels sewn at both shoulders and the sides, and worn belted at the waist. The design is characterized by wide red end borders, often patterned with dark blue terraced motifs, and a solid brown or black center panel. (See Figure 8.)

Dye Any colorant that is absorbed into the fibers of a yarn or fabric or fixed permanently to the fibers by means of a chemical mordant; as opposed to pigments, which are simply painted onto the surface of the fibers and physically adhere to it.

> **Aniline dyes** A family of synthetic dyes of many colors, originally made from a coal-tar derivative called aniline. Anilines were first

synthesized commercially in 1856. The earliest known aniline-dyed yarns in Navajo textiles date to 1863 and were raveled from commercial cloth. Anilines were applied to commercial machine-spun yarns that became readily available in the Southwest during the 1870s, and were sold in powdered form to be applied to Navajo handspun yarns by the 1880s.

Indigo A blue dye, ranging from almost blue-black to pale blue, made from several plants of the genus *Indigofera*. Generally, semiprocessed indigo was imported into the Southwest from Mexico in "lump" form and used by Pueblo, Navajo, and Hispanic weavers to dye their own handspun yarns.

Cochineal A crimson red dye made from the dried, crushed bodies of tiny insects from Mexico, Java, and the Canary Islands. Although the Navajo never used cochineal dye on their own handspun yarns, they raveled red cochineal-dyed yarns from imported fabrics and rewove these yarns into their own fabrics. Cochineal is also found in combination with another insect dye, lac.

Lac A crimson red dye derived from a resinous substance secreted by the scale insect, *Laccifer lacca*. The Navajo raveled yarns dyed with lac (and cochineal/lac combinations) from imported cloths and rewove these yarns into their own blankets. The earliest lac-dyed yarns found in Navajo textiles are raveled yarns that date to about 1800. In mid-nineteenth century raveled yarns, lac is frequently found in combination with cochineal. Around 1860, soon after the invention of synthetic dyes, lac all but disappears from Navajo textiles.

Native dyes Natural dyes that are found, cultivated, and applied in the Southwest; non-synthetic dyes.

Natural dye Dyes of vegetal, animal, or mineral origins; non-synthetic dyes.

Synthetic dye Chemically manufactured dyes. There are many families of synthetic dyes, including aniline dyes.

Vegetal dyes Dyes that use plant materials—leaves, flowers, twigs, bark, and roots—as the chief source of color.

Embroidery Ornamental needlework on fabric. (See Figure 5).

Ends The edges of a textile that parallel the warp selvages; each rectangular textile has two ends and two sides.

Eye-dazzler A bright pattern of small, serrate triangles and diamonds in intense, contrasting colors; the combination "dazzles" the eye. Most eye-dazzlers were woven between 1880 and 1910 from Germantown yarns, although some were woven from handspun yarns colored with synthetic dyes, and some were produced into the mid-twentieth century. (See Figure 13.)

Face Every simple fabric has two faces or surfaces.
    Double-faced Two identical faces.
    Single-faced Only one face is meant to be displayed.
    Two-faced The two faces are dissimilar.

Fleece The coat of wool that covers a sheep.

Germantown yarn *see* Yarn

Handspun yarn *see* Yarn

Hispanic An ethnic designation pertaining to people with cultural origins from Spain.

Hopi brocade Also called extra-weft wrapping; not a true brocade, but an extra-weft patterned fabric on a plain weave ground, in which colored wool wefts pass successively over groups of warps, wrapping around the last pair of each group before progressing across the fabric to form a solid colored pattern. (See Figure 5, 6 and 17).

Join *see* Tapestry weave under Weave

Late Classic Period *see* Classic period of Navajo weaving

Lazy line A subtle diagonal break in the weave of many Navajo fabrics where a weaver has worked on adjacent sections of warps at different times; usually spaced apart no more than the length of the batten, lazy lines allow a weaver to weave a wide fabric without having to reach from side to side with each pass of the weft. Navajo,

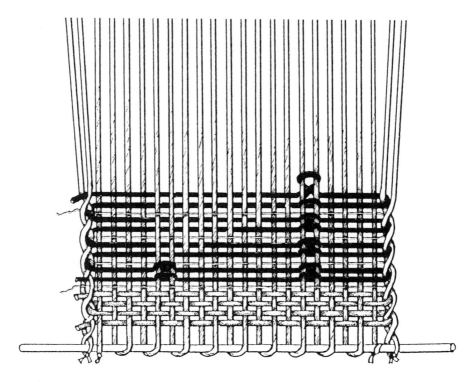

Figure 17. The Hopi brocade technique. Adapted from Kent (1986) by Craig Hansen.

Zuni, and Mayó Indian weavers are the only ones in the Southwest who use lazy lines; neither Hopi nor Hispanic weavers use them.

> *The use of lazy lines goes clear back into the 1700s, so [Navajo weavers] were capable of making pure serrate designs in a very early time period, but they didn't. Lazy lines will cut right straight across the patterns as well as across the background.*

Longer than wide A reference to fabric that is woven with its length in the warp direction greater than its width in the weft direction (across the loom). Note: length always refers to the dimension in the warp direction and width always refers to the dimension in the weft direction.

Manta A garment consisting of a rectangular fabric worn draped over the shoulders as a shawl or around the body as a dress, generally worn by women. Pueblo and Navajo mantas may be plain weave or twill weaves, and are woven in a variety of patterns and colors. (See Plates 2 and 5, and Figures 5 and 7.)

Meander A linear pattern in which the design element moves in a sinuous or winding, albeit usually rectilinear, fashion. Related to the Greek fret or key pattern. (See Figure 11.)

Merino wool *see* Wool

Modern Produced since 1940.

Moki stripes (also spelled Moqui) A design of alternating black (or brown) and dark blue bands used alone or interspersed with white and/or red bands, sometimes with a superimposed design of diamonds and other geometric motifs. The term Moki derives from the Spanish name for the Hopi Indians. The Hopi rarely made blankets patterned with this type of design, although Navajo and Spanish Colonial weavers commonly employ it.

Natural color The color of undyed, untreated wool, cotton, or other textile fibers.

Native dye *see* Dye

Navajo An ethnic designation pertaining to a group of Native Americans who arrived in the American Southwest sometime since the fourteenth century, speak an Athapascan language, and who now live principally on a reservation in parts of northeastern Arizona, northwestern New Mexico and southern Utah.

Nine-spot pattern A chief blanket and sarape style in which bars, diamonds or other geometric motifs are arranged in three rows with three figures in each row. In some textiles the center row may be split into two opposing rows, in which case the design becomes a "twelve spot" pattern.

One-piece dress *see* Dress

Plain weave *see* Weave

Pictorial A textile with depictions of people, animals, birds, land-scapes, vehicles and any other realistic or semi-realistic images woven into the design. (See Figure 14.)

Ply One continuous strand of spun fibers. In multiple-ply yarns, two or more strands of single-ply yarn are twisted together to form a heavier, stronger yarn. (See Figure 18).

Pound blanket/rug A thickly spun, loosely woven textile, generally with a simple design in few colors. Most pound blankets or rugs were woven around 1885-1910 and were sold to traders who paid for them by the pound; this practice continued in some areas into the 1940s and later.

Pueblo An ethnic designation pertaining to several groups of southwestern Native Americans that include the prehistoric Anasazi and the historic and modern peoples of Hopi, Zuni, Acoma, and Laguna (the western Pueblos) and the Tewa-, Tiwa-, Tanoan-, and Keres-speaking (eastern Pueblo) Indian villages along the Rio Grande in New Mexico.

Raveled yarn *see* Yarn

Saddle blanket A blanket that is placed beneath a horse's saddle to prevent the saddle from galling the animal. Single saddle blankets normally measure thirty inches square; double saddle blankets are approximately thirty by sixty inches and are folded in half when used. Saddle blankets are also frequently used as small rugs.

Saddle cover A small textile for use on top of a saddle to cushion the seat and to decorate it; generally less heavy and more decorative than a saddle blanket; often woven in Germantown yarns and adorned along at least one edge with fringe and large tassels.

Sash belt A long, relatively narrow fabric woven in a warp float pattern weave and worn as a belt around the waist; usually red with green and black (Hopi style) or with green and white (Navajo style). The term, sash belt, is one used by Pueblo and Navajo people, and so is adopted here.

Saltillo style An elaborate blanket style of the eighteenth and nineteenth centuries, named for the city of Saltillo, Coahuila, in northwestern Mexico. Important features include serrate patterns, concentric diamonds, center-dominant designs, and vertical background schemes. These elements were adopted by Spanish Colonial weavers of New Mexico and further copied or modified by Navajo weavers after 1870. (See Plate 9.)

Sarape *see* Blanket

Saxony yarn *see* Yarn

Selvage The edge of a fabric where the wefts loop around the side warps and reenter the fabric to weave in the reverse direction and where, as in Navajo and Pueblo textiles that typically have four complete selvages (two warp selvages and two weft selvages), the warps are uncut and loop around the end wefts. *Also spelled* selvedge.

Selvage cords Two or more yarns that twist about each other while interlacing with and reinforcing a fabric's edge. In Navajo textiles, two 3-ply selvage cords are usually twined together, forming a 2-strand edge. In Pueblo fabrics, three 2-ply cords usually form a 3-strand, twined selvage. There are also other variations. (See Figure 19.)

Serape *see* Blanket

Serrate design A pattern of diagonals formed by sharply pointed zigzag lines, frequently used on diamond shapes and other geometric figures. (See Plate 10 and Figure 13.)

Sides The edges of a textile that border the weft selvages; each rectangular textile has two sides and two ends.

Shoulder blanket *see* Blanket

Slit joins *see* Tapestry weave under Weave

Spanish Colonial An ethnic designation pertaining to people with cultural origins from Spain who colonized major parts of the Western as well as areas of the Eastern Hemispheres.

Spider Woman's Cross A cross-shaped motif with small squares or other geometric motifs appended to each outer corner at the cross's

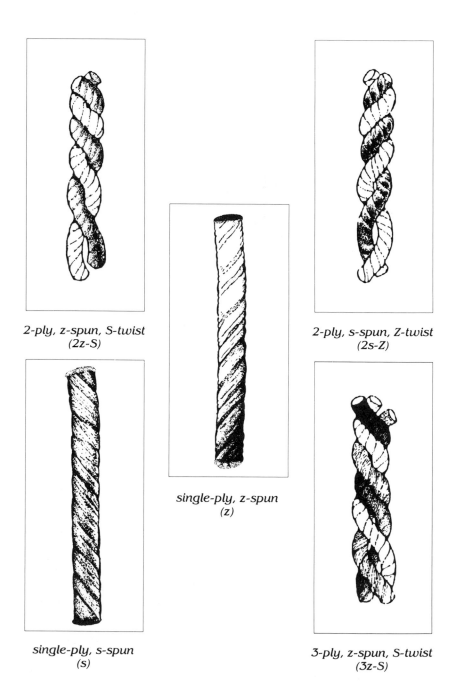

2-ply, z-spun, S-twist
(2z-S)

2-ply, s-spun, Z-twist
(2s-Z)

single-ply, z-spun
(z)

single-ply, s-spun
(s)

3-ply, z-spun, S-twist
(3z-S)

Figure 18. Single and plied yarns. Adapted from Kent (1985) by
Craig Hansen.

Pueblo*: 3-strand twining with 2-ply cords (3 2z-S).

Navajo*: 2-strand twining with 3-ply cords (2 3z-S).

Figure 19. The twined selvage cord technique. Adapted from Emery (1966) by Craig Hansen.

---

*Predominant selvage types only; individual textiles may vary considerably.

arms. Named after Spider Woman, who taught the Navajo to weave, according to Navajo mythology; however, the term may have been coined originally by a trader or other outsider and not by a Navajo. (See Figures 7 and 8.)

Spider Woman's Hole A small, woven-in slit occasionally seen in or near the center of Classic and Late Classic blankets. Frequently, such a slit is finished with twined selvage cords in the same manner as the textile's edges. Named after Spider Woman, who taught the Navajo to weave, according to Navajo mythology; however, the term may have been coined originally by a trader or other outsider and not by a Navajo. Associated with similar purposes as the "Weaver's Pathway."

Spinning The process of drawing out and twisting a group of relatively short fibers into a continuous strand to form a yarn or thread. The two possible directions of spin are noted by the letters S and Z because the angle of spin in a yarn can be represented by the slanting direction of the central portion of each letter. (See Figure 18.) The following notation is used:

z or s Single-ply z-spun or s-spun yarn.
Z or S Direction of final twist of a multiple-ply yarn; when used alone, indicates that the number of plies and direction of spin for each ply have not been determined; if the number of plies is known, the notation may read 3S, 2Z, and so forth;
z-S z-spun, S-twist, two-ply yarn; comparable notations are z-Z, s-Z, and s-S;
3z-S z-spun, S-twist, three-ply yarn; comparable notations are 4z-S, 3s-Z, and so forth. (Kent 1985:117).

All native spun yarn in the Southwest is z-spun, and a good bit of the raveled yarn, particularly the late raveled yarn, is also Z. But if it is s-spun, it is almost certainly raveled yarn. At least 99 percent of all s-spun yarn in the Southwest was raveled.

Spirit line *see* Weaver's pathway

Stripe A design element that extends across a textile in the direction of its warps and parallel to its side selvages; opposed to a band, which is oriented horizontally, following the direction of the wefts.

Synthetic dyes *see* Dye

Tapestry weave *see* Weave

Terraced Stepped design elements that often form rectilinear diagonals, as in terraced triangles, diamonds, and zigzags. (See Plate 3, 4, and 6.)

Trade cloth Commercially manufactured fabric, imported into the Southwest

Transitional period (1880–1900) A time when the production of Navajo blankets made for native consumption and for trade to other peoples who would wear them was changing to the production of rugs, other home furnishings, and souvenirs for sale to outsiders. Weaving of this period is characterized by the use of many new materials (a continuation of the Late Classic trend), Germantown yarns, bright colors, bordered patterns, and heavier spinning and weaving in order to conform to the requirements of a carpet rather than a wearing blanket.

Tufted A weaving technique in which extra pieces of yarn or long fibers are inserted into the background fabric during the process of weaving, producing a shaggy pile effect.

Twelve-spot pattern A chief blanket and sarape style in which bars, diamonds, or other geometric motifs are arranged in four rows with three figures in each row. Related to the "nine-spot pattern."

Twill *see* Weave

Twining A weaving technique in which pairs (or more) of yarns twist around each other while enclosing a second set of yarns within each turn or half-turn. In Pueblo and Navajo weaving, all four selvages often have a set of selvage cords that are twined about each other while enclosing either the looped warps or wefts, depending upon whether it is the warp or weft selvage. (See Selvage and Figure 19.)

Two-piece dress *see* Dress

Vallero star An eight pointed star motif often depicted in several alternating colors. Named for the Rio Grande Valley from which many

Spanish Colonial blankets using this motif came, although Navajo and other weavers use it too. It is presumed by some to be derived originally from a pattern frequently seen in early American patchwork quilts. (*See* Plate 8.)

Vegetal dye *see* Dye

Warp The parallel yarns that are strung on a loom and form the foundation onto which the weft yarns are woven.

> **Continuous warp** A weaving system in which a warp yarn is wound back and forth across the loom frame so as to create a "closed system" with no cut threads; used to produce an uncut four-selvage fabric such as that made by Pueblo and Navajo weavers, and also produced on backstrap looms from other parts of the world.

Weave To interlace yarns together to form a fabric. (See Emery 1966.)

> **Balanced weave** Warps and wefts are the same size and equally spaced.
>
> **Plain weave** Each weft passes over one warp, then under the next warp in a regular sequence.
>
> **Weft-faced weave** Wefts conceal the warps.
>
> **Warp-faced weave** Warps conceal the wefts.
>
> **Tapestry weave** A weft-faced plain weave in which differently colored pattern areas are formed by wefts worked in separate sections; weft-faced plain weave with discontinuous wefts. There are many ways of connecting adjacent color areas:
>
> > **Join** Refers to line where a color change is made between two design elements. (See Figure 20.)
> >
> > **Slit tapestry join** Wefts turn around adjacent warps and create a slit between the color areas; they do not interlock or dovetail but remain independent of each other.

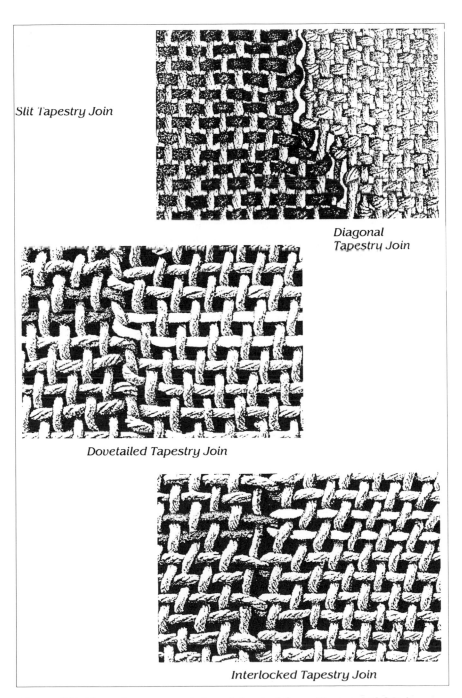

Figure 20. Tapestry weave joins. Adapted from Emery (1966) by Craig Hansen.

Diagonal tapestry join Related to the slit joins but the join is progressively offset along a diagonal line; wefts do not turn around each other. The resulting slits between colors are small and inconspicuous.

Interlocked tapestry join Wefts of adjacent color areas are linked together by turning around each other between adjacent warps.

Dovetailed tapestry join Wefts of adjacent color areas are connected by turning around a common warp and not by turning around each other.

> *Dovetailing was the preferred form for Spanish weavers because they were using a shuttle. The Navajo and Pueblo more often used interlocking.*

Twill weave Float weave in which wefts pass over two or more warps and the floats for each successive pass are usually aligned diagonally. (See Plates 2 and 5, Figure 7)
    Diagonal twill weave Floats progress in one direction creating a diagonal texture in the fabric.
    Herringbone twill weave Float diagonals in alternate directions to form a zigzag pattern.
    Diamond twill weave Floats diverge to form a diamond-shaped pattern.
    Modified twill weave Floats have an irregular arrangement and no diagonal alignment results.

Warp float pattern weave Warp-faced technique used by Pueblo and Navajo weavers for making belts, in which some of the warp yarns create a pattern by floating over more than one weft at a time.

Wedge weave (eccentric weave) An unusual weave found in some blankets of the late nineteenth century in which wefts are placed at oblique rather than right angles to the warp to form a series of diagonal, zigzag or diamond patterns. Because the warp yarns are generally forced out of their normal vertical position, the edges of the blanket become scalloped. Also called a "pulled warp weave." (See Plate 7.)

Weaver's pathway A small thin line that extends from the center design field across the border to the outside edge of some rugs; the line is frequently placed near a corner and made of the same color as the center field's background. Also called the spirit line. Associated with the belief of allowing the energy and spirit woven into a particular textile to be released in order for the weaver to have the energy and imagination to continue weaving other textiles.

Wedge weave *see* Weave

Weft The yarns that are interlaced with, that is, woven over and under the warp yarns; the warp and weft yarns are usually placed at right angles to each other.

Wider than long A reference to fabric that is woven with its width in the weft direction (across the loom) greater than its length in the warp direction. Note: width always refers to the dimension in the weft direction and length always refers to the dimension in the warp direction.

Wool Curly fibers that form the fleece of sheep.

> **Churro wool** A soft, long, lustrous wool with little grease or crimp, easy to work by hand. The churro breed of sheep was originally brought from Andalusia to the Southwest by the Spanish in 1598. This wool appears most frequently in blankets made before the 1880s.

> **Merino wool** Wool from a Spanish sheep breed introduced by the United States government during the 1880s along with the French Rambouillet breed. These short, curly, and greasy wools were difficult to work by hand but superior for producing textiles by machine.

Yarn Cordage made of fibers twisted together in a continuous length.

> **Commercial yarn** Machine-spun yarns, usually industrially dyed; manufactured by a non native industrial process and obtained through a trading post, store, or other outlet of commerce.

> **Germantown yarn** Commercial 3-ply and 4-ply American-manufactured yarn colored with aniline dyes; originally made in Ger-

mantown, Pennsylvania. Three-ply yarns were issued to the Navajos beginning in 1864 and replaced by 4-ply versions around 1875. Both types were colored with a wide range of synthetic dyes and used in Transitional Period blankets, rugs, pillow covers, and other novelty items. The use of 4-ply Germantown yarns was discouraged by traders after 1900 but persisted well into the twentieth century anyway. The Pueblos also used Germantown yarns in their embroidery, brocade weaves, and sash belts.

Handspun yarn Usually a yarn of native manufacture, spun on a shaft-and-whorl hand spindle or on a hand- or treadle-operated spinning wheel. In contrast to industrial machine-spun yarns, which are designated as commercial.

Raveled yarn Yarn obtained by unweaving a fabric by separating the warps and wefts. These yarns can then be rewoven directly into another fabric, or can be carded and respun to form entirely different yarns. *See also* Bayeta.

Saxony yarn Fine 3-ply yarn spun from the wool of merino sheep and dyed with natural dyes. These yarns were produced in Saxony, a former German state, and in England, France, and New England during the first half of the nineteenth century. After 1821, Saxony yarns were imported to the Southwest by way of the Santa Fe Trail. They were used by the Spanish for color accents and, about mid-century, by the Navajos for general weaving. In southwestern weaving, most Saxony yarn is limited to one shade of red.

Anything 3-ply was called Saxony in the early days, but it ain't.

Zoned bands *see* Banded

Further Reading

Emery, Irene
    1966   *The Primary Structures of Fabrics.* Washington, D.C.:
    The Textile Museum

Kent, Kate Peck
    1983a   *Prehistoric Textiles of the Southwest.* Albuquerque:
    University of New Mexico Press.

    1983b   *Pueblo Indian Textiles: A Living Tradition.* Santa Fe,
    NM: School of American Research Press.

    1985   *Navajo Weaving: Three Centuries of Change.* Santa Fe,
    NM: School of American Research Press.

Mera, H.P.
    1987   *Spanish-American Blanketry: Its Relationship to
    Aboriginal Weaving in the Southwest.* Santa Fe: School of
    American Research Press.

Museum of International Folk Art
    1979   *Spanish Textile Tradition of New Mexico and Colorado.*
    Santa Fe: Museum of New Mexico Press.

Reichard, Gladys
    1934   *Spider Woman.* New York: Macmillan. (Reprinted as
    Weaving a Navajo Blanket by Dover, New York, 1974).

    1936   *Navajo Shepherd and Weaver.* New York: J.J. Augustin.
    (Reprinted by Rio Grande Press, Glorieta, NM, 1968).

    1939   *Dezba, Woman of the Desert.* New York: J.J. Augustin.

Wheat, Joe Ben

1976a   Navajo Textiles. In *Fred Harvey Fine Arts Collection*. Pp. 9-47. Phoenix, AZ: The Heard Museum.

1976b   Spanish-American and Navajo Weaving, 1600 to Now. In *Collected Papers in Honor of Margery Ferguson Lambert*. A. Schroeder, ed. Papers of the Archaeological Society of New Mexico 3:199-226.

1977   Documentary Basis for Material Changes and Design Styles in Navajo Blanket Weaving. In *Ethnographic Textiles of the Western Hemisphere*, 1977 Proceedings of the Irene Emery Roundtable on Museum Textiles. Irene Emery and Patricia Fiske, eds. Pp. 420-440. Washington, D.C.: The Textile Museum.

1981   Early Navajo Weaving. *Plateau* 52(4):2-9. Museum of Northern Arizona, Flagstaff, AZ.

1984   *The Gift of Spiderwoman: Southwestern Textiles, The Navajo Tradition*. Philadelphia: The University Museum, University of Pennsylvania.